THIS BOOK BELONGS TO

. . . .

To Uncle Peter, who loves the great outdoors.
E.J.

To Laura, with thanks for the colour chart idea in November!
A.W.

First published 2020 by Nosy Crow Ltd.
The Crow's Nest, 14 Baden Place, Crosby Row
London SE1 1YW
www.nosycrow.com

ISBN 978 1 78800 821 1

'The National Trust' and the oak leaf logo are registered trademarks of The National Trust
(Enterprises) Limited (a subsidiary of The National Trust for Places of
Historic Interest or Natural Beauty, Registered Charity Number 205846)

Nosy Crow and associated logos are trademarks and/or registered trademarks of Nosy Crow Ltd.

Text © Anna Wilson 2018, 2019, 2020
Illustrations © Elly Jahnz 2018, 2019, 2020

The right of Anna Wilson to be identified as the author and Elly Jahnz
to be identified as the illustrator of this work has been asserted.

A CIP catalogue record for this book is available from the British Library.

Printed in China

Papers used by Nosy Crow are made from wood grown in sustainable forests.

1 3 5 7 9 8 6 4 2

2021
NATURE
MONTH-BY-MONTH

 A Children's Almanac

Anna Wilson   Elly Jahnz

WHAT IS AN ALMANAC?

The first almanacs were created about 3,000 years ago!
They were written by the ancient Egyptians, who used
a kind of paper made from reeds known as papyrus.
The writers listed all the dates that were thought to
be lucky or unlucky, and made predictions about the
weather. Farmers used these almanacs to help them
know when to plant seeds and when to harvest crops.

Nowadays you can also find almanacs (like this one!)
which have fun facts about each month – things to
do indoors and outdoors, animals to spot, festivals to
celebrate and seasonal food to grow, cook and eat.
They also contain information about the weather,
the night sky and all sorts of other amazing facts.

WARNING!

This book contains activities which involve
things like knives, saws, hammers and nails
and hot ovens. There are also a lot of fun
things to do outside which involve fire and
very cold water! All the activities are safe if
you are sensible, follow safety guidelines and
take a grown-up along to look out for you.

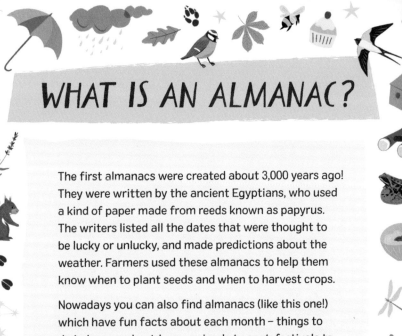

CONTENTS

JANUARY

SPECIAL DAYS

1st New Year's Day/First-footing

5th Twelfth Night/Wassailing

6th Epiphany

13th Lohri (Punjabi midwinter festival)

25th Burns Night

28th Tu B'Shevat (Jewish New Year)

ANNIVERSARIES

45 years ago...

The writer Agatha Christie lived from 15 September 1890 to 12 January 1976. She is famous for her gripping crime thrillers, such as *Murder on the Orient Express* which was made into a film in 1974 and 2017.

80 years ago...

The pilot Amy Johnson lived from 1 July 1903 to 5 January 1941. She was famous for trying to set a world record for flying solo from London to Darwin, Australia. She set many long-distance records during the 1930s and she also flew in the Second World War.

*"January brings the snow,
Makes our feet and fingers glow."*

SARA COLERIDGE (1802–1852)

January can be a dull and dreary month after the excitement of Christmas and New Year's Eve – unless it snows of course! Who doesn't love a 'snow day'? Even if it doesn't snow, there are still lots of lovely things you can do, both outdoors and indoors, this month. You could wrap up warm and go for a walk to see what you can find. Yes, the trees are bare, but you should still be able to spot birds and other creatures out in the park or garden. There are also some wonderful festivals this month which offer a good excuse for getting friends round or throwing a party. So maybe January is not so dull after all!

Why is January Called January?

The calendar we use today was invented by the Romans. January was named after the Roman god Janus who was the god of gates and doorways. He was always drawn with two faces looking in opposite directions – one face looked back at the year that had passed, and the other looked forwards into the new year.

New Year's Resolutions

On 31st December we often talk about 'making resolutions' for the new year. Why do we do this?

The tradition of making resolutions started with the Romans, too. Because the January god, Janus, was looking backwards and forwards at the same time, he became a symbol for the Romans of forgetting what had happened in the past and moving on into the future. January therefore became known as a month in which to forgive people and be kind.

Nowadays, people seem to worry more about getting fit and not eating chocolate – maybe we should be more like the Romans and make resolutions to be kinder instead?

Here are some ideas for resolutions that you might manage to keep . . .

- Look out for someone at school who needs a friend.
- Have a cake sale or organise a sponsored silence or a sponsored walk for charity.
- Clear out your old toys and clothes and take them to a charity shop. (Check with an adult before you give these things away!)
- Help out around the house and/or garden, if you have one.

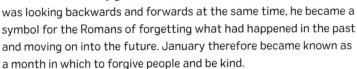

DID YOU KNOW...

January starts on the same day of the week as October and ends on the same day of the week as February and October. If it's a leap year, January starts on the same day of the week as April and July and ends on the same day of the week as July.

FESTIVAL FUN

The colourful festivals of light such as Christmas, Hanukkah and Diwali might be over, but January has its fair share of celebrations to look forward to.

5th January *Twelfth Night*

For Christians, Twelfth Night used to be the day when Christmas was celebrated. In some countries, 6th January is still the day on which children get their presents. It is also known as Epiphany, St Nicholas's Day and the Feast of the Three Kings.

5th January *Wassailing*

Wassailing is a pagan tradition. The word *wassail* comes from the Anglo-Saxon words *waes hael* which mean 'good health'. The festival looks forward to what people hope for in the new year to come: good weather, good health and a good harvest.

Wassailing involves going out into the countryside to bless the apple trees. The wassail king and queen lead everyone in a sing-song around the tree to encourage it to produce lots of apples.

13th January *Lohri*

Hindus and Sikhs all over the world celebrate Lohri. During Lohri, songs are sung to the sun god, Surya, thanking him for his warmth and praying for his return after the cold weather.

People drink *jaggery* – a delicious sugary drink made from sugar cane. *Gajak* is also eaten – a thin, dry sweet made from roasted sesame seeds cooked in sugary syrup and spices. Children go from house to house singing folk songs and are given sweets. In the evening, a bonfire is lit and people gather together to dance.

Recipe for *Gajak*

This delicious crunchy sweet is made and eaten during the festival of Lohri, as well as at the similar festivals of Makar Sankranti and Pongal, which are celebrated around the same date. Ask an adult to help you make this treat as the sugary syrup, or *jaggery*, gets very hot!

You will need:

Rectangular ovenproof dish (about 23 cm x 35 cm)
Greaseproof paper
Heavy-bottomed frying pan
Tablespoon
Saucepan
Wooden spoon
Rolling pin
Sharp knife

2 tablespoons of ghee, plus extra for greasing
125 g sesame seeds
200 g caster sugar
2 tablespoons of water

Allergy warning: this recipe contains sesame seeds.

1. Grease the ovenproof dish with some of the ghee and put it to one side.
2. Put the sesame seeds into the frying pan and toast them (with no oil or fat) on a low heat until they start to turn brown. Put them on a plate and leave to one side while you make the syrup.
3. Mix the sugar and ghee with 2 tablespoons of water in the saucepan.
4. Cook the mixture on a medium heat until it turns thick and syrupy.
5. Take the pan off the heat and, using the wooden spoon, fold in the roasted sesame seeds.
6. Once everything is well mixed, pour the sweet treat into the greased ovenproof dish and smooth it flat with the rolling pin. Let it cool completely.
7. Leave until the mixture is cool and firm, then ask an adult to cut it into rectangles with the sharp knife. Or you can have a go at snapping it with your fingers if you don't mind odd shapes!

OUTDOOR ADVENTURES

It can be very hard to get up in the mornings in January. The sun doesn't seem to appear until school has begun – if it appears at all! But the dark mornings can be an exciting time for spotting wildlife. Even if you are not lucky enough to see an animal or bird, you might hear one instead if you listen hard.

Owls become very noisy at this time of year. You might catch sight of the large, silent shape of a tawny owl or a barn owl flying past you on your way to school.

Foxes and badgers are busy at this time of year, too. They have to work hard to find food to keep them alive through the cold winter. Sometimes you can see them knocking over rubbish bins in their search for food!

If you go out into the garden, the park or the woods near where you live, you will see signs of new life even on the darkest day. In colder northern regions, plants take longer to appear, while down in the south you might see daffodils as early as 1st January.

Snowdrops are already in bloom in January. Their tiny white and green heads look so delicate, but they are strong enough to survive the coldest weather – even snow and ice!

Other plants are quietly peeping out of the damp, dark ground, too. Hazel catkins can be seen hanging from the trees, even before the leaves start to show their shoots. Sometimes little yellow primroses start to appear now.

Make a *Nature Notebook*

1 Take some sheets of scrap paper, fold them in half to make a booklet, then staple them together where you've made the fold.

2 Remember to make the notebook small enough to fit into a pocket so that you can take it with you wherever you go.

3 Tie a piece of string to a pencil and stick the loose end of the string into the notebook with sticky tape or make a hole in the pages and thread the string through. Use the pencil to note down where and when you see things while you are out and about.

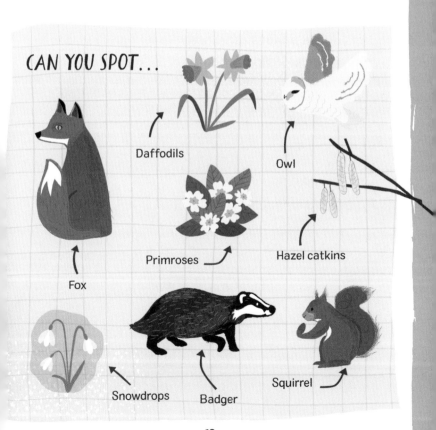

CAN YOU SPOT...

Daffodils

Owl

Primroses

Hazel catkins

Fox

Snowdrops

Badger

Squirrel

THE SEASIDE IN WINTER

Maybe a trip to the seaside is not at the top of your list of things to do at this time of the year! It's true that it's too chilly to go for a swim or a paddle, as the sea temperature has dropped to between 6°C and 10°C at this time of year. However, you can still have fun hunting for shells, pebbles, seaweed and fossils. And there are some beautiful seabirds and other creatures for you to spot. Common seals can be seen along the UK coastline, and in Scotland, Wales and Cornwall you might also see porpoises. Wherever you go, make sure you take your nature notebook with you so that you can write down or draw what you see!

CAN YOU SPOT...

Gannet

Shag

Cormorant

Turnstone

Rock pipit

Redshank

Oystercatcher

Curlew

Take a bucket and a net with you, too. The weather may not be good enough for you to sit about making sandcastles, but hopping between the rock pools will keep you warm. See how many different objects you can find. The winter storms bring in all sorts of treasures, from pretty shells to funny-shaped driftwood to sea-softened pieces of coloured glass. Have a competition with your friends and family – the person with the most items wins. If you're really lucky, you may even find some real buried treasure!

WOOD SCULPTURES

If you do go to the seaside, look out for small pieces of driftwood. Driftwood is any kind of wood that the tides have brought in. It is usually beautifully soft because the waves throw it around and bash it against the rocks, so it tends not to have splinters or sharp edges. You'll need to take it home and dry it out before trying to make anything from it.

If you don't get to the seaside, you can still make sculptures from sticks that you can find in the park or the woods. You'll need to dry them out, too, before you use them. The strongest glue to use is special wood glue – you'll need to ask an adult to help you with that. Sometimes PVA glue works just as well, especially if the wood is very dry.

Have a go at making a sculpture by gluing stacks of different-sized wood pieces together. Or what about covering an old photo or mirror frame with smaller pieces? If you are feeling very adventurous, take a look at what other sculptors have made from wood, such as the amazing horses made by artist Heather Jansch at the Eden Project in Cornwall. That would keep you busy on a cold, dark January afternoon!

BIRD SPOTTING

The RSPB holds a survey called the Big Garden Birdwatch at the end of January every year. This is to encourage people to record the different types of birds that regularly visit our gardens and streets so that we can keep an eye on their habits and see how the weather has affected them. More than half a million people get involved every year. Check the RSPB website to see how you can get involved. **www.rspb.org.uk**

CAN YOU SPOT...

Blue tit

Coal tit

Long-tailed tit

Wren

Great tit

Blackbird

House Sparrow

Starling

Robin

Magpie

Goldfinch

Wood pigeon

THE NIGHT SKY

If there are no clouds, January is a great time for stargazing. As it gets dark so early, you can wrap up warm and go outside to look at the night sky.

Sometimes we see only part of the moon, depending on where the moon is in its journey across the sky. The different stages of this journey are called the 'phases of the moon'.

Phases of the Moon in January 2021

Last Quarter
6th January

New Moon
13th January

First Quarter
20th January

Full Moon
28th January

The full moon in January is known as the Wolf Moon.

WINTER WALKS

It is tempting not to go outside at all in January if you can help it! However, often it's better to be out in the cold than to be inside staring miserably at it through the window.

'Poohsticks' is a good game for this time of year as the rivers and streams are usually quite high and so the water is flowing fast.

Poohsticks

This game comes from the lovely stories of the bear Winnie-the-Pooh by A. A. Milne. Pooh plays the game with his friends Christopher Robin and Piglet.

1 *First, you need to find a narrow bridge over a stream or river. Then you need to find a small stick for each person who wants to play.*

2 *Line up along the bridge, facing the flow of the river – in other words, the water should be flowing towards you and running under the bridge away from you.*

3 *Hold your sticks over the edge. Be very careful not to lean too far!*

4 *Choose one person to be the judge – they must say, "Ready, steady, go!" and then everyone drops their stick straight down into the river. Do not cheat by throwing your stick under the bridge!*

5 *Run to the other side of the bridge and watch the sticks come out. The first one to appear is the winner!*

FEBRUARY

SPECIAL DAYS

1st Imbolc (pagan celebration)

2nd Candlemas (Christian festival)

12th Chinese New Year (Year of the Ox)

14th St Valentine's Day

16th Shrove Tuesday (Pancake Day)

17th Ash Wednesday (Christian festival)

26th Purim (Jewish festival)

ANNIVERSARIES

90 years ago ...

On 14 February 1931, *The Highway Code* was first published. This is the book of rules about driving that everyone must read when they learn to drive.

180 years ago ...

On 25 February 1841, the French painter Pierre-Auguste Renoir was born. He was known for his 'impressionist' paintings of people in Paris.

> *"Late February days;*
> *and now at last, Might you have*
> *thought that Winter's woe was passed."*

WILLIAM MORRIS (1834–1896)

February starts off cold and dark – at first it seems even more wintry than January! But by the end of the month we will have two hours more daylight and spring will be around the corner.

People often think of February as a time to be quiet and thoughtful before nature wakes up from its long winter's sleep. A few religions hold a 'fast' during this month, which means that people do not eat anything during daylight hours. Some Christians fast during Lent, which often occurs in February. Buddhists fast during a full moon. Some pagans fast in preparation for Ostara, the spring festival. The idea is that fasting helps you to clear your mind and focus on prayer.

By the middle of February, we can feel tired and in need of a break – so it's a good thing that the half-term holidays happen this month!

Why is February Called February?

The Latin name for this month was *Februarius*. It came from the Latin word *februum* which means 'purification'. The Romans thought of the fifth day of this month as the official first day of spring. On the fifteenth they celebrated a festival called *Februa*.

This was a time to get rid of evil spirits and to cleanse the air so that people felt fit and healthy for spring. This is where we get our idea of spring cleaning from. Perhaps you could use the colder, darker days this month to tidy your bedroom or help clear out the shed or garage.

FEBRUARY BIRTH SIGNS

Aquarius

The sign of the water-carrier. Some people believe that if you have your birthday between 20th January and 18th February, then this is your sign. You are supposed to be an inquisitive and logical person who does not like to follow rules just for the sake of it.

Pisces

This is the sign of the fish. If you were born between 19th February and 20th March, then you are a Piscean. Some people believe this means you are very emotional, creative and good at working out things based on your feelings.

DID YOU KNOW...

Before the Romans changed the calendar, the length of February used to change a lot. At one point it had only 23 days. The Anglo-Saxons called February *Solmonath*, which means 'the month of cakes'. This is because cakes and bread were offered to the gods to make sure that there would be a good harvest that year.

FESTIVAL FUN

February is not all about fasting, cleaning and staying quiet. There are lots of celebrations happening all around the world, too. Some have serious meanings, but others are good fun!

1st February *Imbolc*

Imbolc (pronounced 'imulk') is a pagan festival. Its name comes from the Celtic word *imbolg* which means 'in the belly'. This is because nature seems to be expecting lots of babies at this time of year – baby animals, baby trees, baby flowers and fruit and vegetables. Everything is hidden away at the moment, but that doesn't mean nothing is happening deep in the cold, dark ground – or inside pregnant animals! To celebrate, people sometimes make dolls made of corn called 'Bridey dolls' which are said to bring good luck.

2nd February *Candlemas*

Candlemas is a Christian festival. It celebrates the day that the baby Jesus was taken to the temple for the first time. The festival always takes place on 2nd February and marks the end of the Christmas season. At Ripon Cathedral in Yorkshire, people celebrate by lighting 5,000 candles to symbolise Jesus bringing light into the darkness of the world.

12th February *Chinese New Year*

2021 is the Year of the Ox. People born under this sign are believed to be cautious and hard-working. Every Ox year has an element attached to it: either Wood, Fire, Earth, Metal or Water. 2021 is the year of the Metal Ox. People born this year are believed to be especially determined.

14th February *St Valentine's Day*

St Valentine's Day is an ancient tradition. Today, it's seen as a day to celebrate love. People send cards and flowers (particularly red roses), chocolates and other gifts. In some parts of Norfolk and Suffolk there is an old custom of leaving presents on people's doorsteps on St Valentine's Eve, the night before St Valentine's Day.

16th February *Shrove Tuesday (Pancake Day)*

Shrove Tuesday gets its name from the ancient Christian practice of being 'shriven', which means being forgiven for things you've done wrong. It was traditional to tell a priest about anything bad you had done to get it out of the way before Lent, the season of fasting. Then, during the fast, you could concentrate on asking for forgiveness and promising to live a better life. On Shrove Tuesday, people used up eggs and fatty foods because during Lent they were not allowed to eat these things. One of the best ways of using up eggs and fat is to make pancakes, and a lot of people still do this today. That is why we also call this day Pancake Day.

17th February *Ash Wednesday*

Ash Wednesday is the first day of Lent. After all the pancake-eating and feasting, it is a quieter, more serious day. Christians spend the time thinking about how to live a better life and looking forward to Easter. Some people go to church and the priest or vicar draws a cross on their foreheads in ash. This is to remember that Jesus died on the cross to save them from the things they had done wrong.

26th February *Purim*

Purim begins on the evening of 25th and ends on the evening of 26th March. It is a Jewish holiday during which Jewish people remember that long ago their people were saved from Haman, a cruel man who worked for the King of Persia. At Purim, people have a big feast and send money and gifts of food to people in need. It is a time to think of others and be thankful for a good life.

Recipe for *Perfect Pancakes*

Why not have a pancake race in your local park with your friends? Dress up in silly costumes and see who can run the fastest while holding a pancake in a frying pan. Whoever drops their pan or pancake is out of the race.

You will need:

Large mixing bowl
Whisk
Frying pan
Palette knife
Ladle
Kitchen paper

100 g plain flour
Pinch of salt
2 eggs
300 ml semi-skimmed milk
1 tablespoon of sunflower or vegetable oil plus extra for frying

1 *Put the flour and salt into the mixing bowl. Make a small dip in the centre with your fingers, then crack the eggs into it.*

2 *Pour in about 50 ml milk and all of the oil. Start whisking from the centre.*

3 *As you whisk, ask someone to help pour in the rest of the milk. Your batter should be as runny as single cream.*

4 *Grease the inside of the frying pan with oiled kitchen paper.*

5 *Heat the pan over a medium heat.*

6 *Pour one ladleful of batter into the pan. Tilt the pan to move the mixture around, making a thin and even layer.*

7 *Leave to cook for about 30 seconds. The pancake should turn golden underneath.*

8 *Hold the pan handle and gently slide a palette knife under the pancake, then quickly lift it and turn it over.*

9 *Cook the other side for another 30 seconds before turning it on to a warm plate.*

10 *Continue with the rest of the batter, serving the pancakes as you cook. Serve with lemon juice, sugar and melted butter. Or choose your own favourite topping!*

WEATHER

"When halo rings moon or sun,
Rain's approaching on the run."

This is an old country saying, and there is some truth in it. If you see a halo around the moon or sun at this time of year, it is because ice crystals can sometimes form in high clouds. These make a ring or 'halo' appear, and later these crystals may fall as rain. Rainy days can seem boring, but remember that the rain is doing a good job of watering all those tiny plants that are waiting for spring to arrive. Also, the rain comes from clouds which come in all shapes and sizes. Cloud spotting can be fun – what kind of pictures and shapes can you see in the clouds today?

Cloud Spotting

Most of our names for clouds come from Latin. They are a combination of the following:

Stratus/strato =
low, flat/layered and smooth

Cumulus/cumulo =
heaped up/puffy, like cauliflower

Cirrus/cirro =
High up/wispy

Alto =
Medium level

Nimbus/nimbo =
Rain-bearing cloud

Combining the names tells you a bit more about the clouds. For example: nimbus + stratus = 'nimbostratus'. This is a cloud which is flat and layered and will probably bring rain. 'Cumulonimbus' is a puffy cloud which will bring rain, too.

THE SOLAR SYSTEM

The sun is in the middle of the solar system – the Earth and all the planets listed below move around the sun, and the moon moves around the Earth.

Sun   Mercury   Venus   Earth   Mars   Jupiter   Saturn   Uranus   Neptune

Constellation of the Month

Canis Major, or the 'Great Dog', can be seen this month. It chases Orion, the 'Hunter', across the sky. To find it, look for Sirius, the 'Dog Star'. In fact, this is two stars very close together which is why it is so bright. It is one of the closest stars to Planet Earth.

DID YOU KNOW...

The full moon in February was known by Native American tribes as the Snow Moon because the heaviest snows often fell in February.

FEED THE BIRDS

Small birds are hungry at this time of year. They need to eat all day to get enough food to keep them going through the winter. You can help by making your own treats for the birds using food scraps from home.

You don't need to spend a lot of money on fancy feeders or a beautiful bird table. You'll need to buy the bird seed and nuts, but if you buy a big sack from a garden centre it is cheaper than buying small quantities, and it will last a long time. You can also use a surprising amount of food scraps that are easy to find at home. Raisins, sultanas, other dried fruit or unsalted nuts go down well with any wild bird.

Make an *Orange Bird Feeder*

These are very easy and fun to make. And the best thing is, you can make yourself a tasty treat too! Ask an adult to help you cut the oranges in half and then use a juicer or squeezer to make some delicious fresh orange juice. Put it in the fridge and enjoy it as a reward once you have finished making these pretty feeders.

You will need:

Empty orange halves
Shallow oven dish
Wooden spoon
Saucepan
Bird seeds
Raisins
Unsalted nuts
Unsalted nut butter or dairy butter or lard

1. *Pour the seeds, fruit and/or nuts into the dish and give them a good stir with the wooden spoon.*
2. *Scoop up a handful of the bird food and press it into the orange halves.*
3. *Ask an adult to help you melt the fat or spread you have chosen to use.*
4. *Pour the melted fat or spread into the orange cups.*
5. *Use the wooden spoon to gently pat the mixture down into the orange cups. Let it solidify.*
6. *Put them on the bird table or windowsill.*

LET IT SNOW

Although we think of having a 'white Christmas', it's much more likely to snow in February in Britain. If it does this year, you won't have to think hard about the fun you can have outdoors. Everyone loves rushing out to make the first footprints in the snow, catching snowflakes on their tongue, having a snowball fight, sledging or building a snowman.

If you wrap up extra warm, you can make snow angels: lie down in a patch of freshly fallen snow and move your arms and legs up and down in the snow. Get up carefully and look at the pattern left behind – you've made a snow angel!

With a bit of help, you can also build a small igloo by packing the snow up into walls.

Or you can make snow bricks by using a spade to cut chunks of snow into cubes. Remember to leave a gap so that you can crawl inside.

You can also create wonderful snow lanterns by building a pyramid of snowballs and placing a tea light in the middle. Ask an adult to help you light the tea light and put it in the middle of your finished pile of snowballs.

WILDLIFE ON THE MOVE

Toads, frogs and newts are often on the move in February. They walk and hop a long way to find others to breed with. The females then go on another long journey back to their ponds. They follow the same route, year after year. This sometimes gets them into trouble, as they cross roads which were not there hundreds of years ago.

To help prevent the amphibians from getting squashed, there are Toad Patrols up and down the country which go out in the evenings and pick the creatures up and carry them safely across the road. You can help amphibians to migrate safely by joining a patrol near you.

To find a Toad Crossing near you, go to **www.froglife.org** and follow the links. It's good fun and you can do some stargazing and wildlife-watching too as foxes, badgers and owls are out in the evening as well.

CAN YOU SPOT...

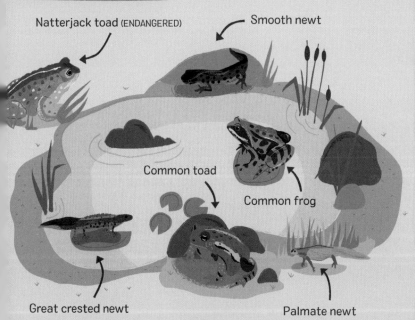

Natterjack toad (ENDANGERED)

Smooth newt

Common toad

Common frog

Great crested newt

Palmate newt

MARCH

SPECIAL DAYS

1st   St David's Day (Wales)
5th   St Piran's Day (Cornwall)
11th   Isra and Mi'raj (Muslim celebration)
14th   Mother's Day
17th   St Patrick's Day (Ireland)
20th   Spring equinox (first day of spring)/Ostara (pagan celebration)
27th   Passover begins (Jewish celebration)
28th   Daylight saving (clocks go forward)
29th   Holi (Hindu festival of colours)

ANNIVERSARIES

150 years ago . . .

On 29 March 1871, Queen Victoria opened the Royal Albert Hall in London. This is where the classical music concerts called the Proms are held every year for eight weeks during the summer.

175 years ago . . .

On 17 March 1846, the artist, writer and children's book illustrator Kate Greenaway was born. The prize known as the Kate Greenaway Medal was named after her in 1955. It is still awarded each year to a children's book illustrator.

> *"It was one of those March days when the sun shines hot and the wind blows cold."*

CHARLES DICKENS (1812–1870)

This quote describes very well how we might look out of the window in March and think, "It looks lovely out there!" only to go outside and find ourselves shivering our socks off! At least the days are getting longer though.

DID YOU KNOW...

Every year March ends on the same day of the week as June.

Why is March Called March?

The Romans called this month *Martius*. It was named after the god of war and farming. That might seem a strange combination, but both war and farming began again in March after the long winter months. Even soldiers didn't like getting cold and wet! The Anglo-Saxons called March *Lentmonath*, which means 'lengthening month', because of the way that the daylight increases during this time. It is also where we get the word 'Lent' from.

Spring Equinox

20th March is the spring equinox. This is one of the days in the year in which the number of hours of daylight is exactly equal to the number of hours of darkness. This happens because the rays of the sun are shining straight at the equator (the middle of the Earth).

Phases of the Moon **in March 2021**

Last Quarter	**New Moon**	**First Quarter**	**Full Moon**
6th March	13th March	21st March	28th March

FESTIVAL FUN

11th March *Isra and Mi'raj*

This festival is in two parts. The first part, the *Isra* or the 'Night Journey', starts on the evening before the day of celebrations. Muslims remember the Prophet Muhammad's journey from Mecca to Jerusalem and then to heaven. Muslim people believe the Night Journey started when the Angel Gabriel took the Prophet Muhammad to Jerusalem on a winged horse, where he met and prayed with prophets including Moses and Jesus.

The second part is the *Mi'raj*, which means 'ladder' in Arabic. This was when the Prophet Muhammad was carried up to heaven by Gabriel where he spoke to Allah (God), who told the Prophet that Muslims should say their prayers five times a day. At Isra and Mi'raj, Muslim people say prayers during the night and Muslim cities keep their lights on all night.

14th March *Mother's Day*

Mother's Day (or Mothering Sunday) always falls on the fourth Sunday in Lent, three weeks before Easter Day. It was originally a Christian festival, and it has now become a day for people to say thank you to their mothers or carers. Why not make a card or promise jar (p. 41) to show your mother or career how much they mean to you?

20th March *Ostara*

Ostara is a pagan festival which is celebrated at the spring equinox. For pagans, it's a time of year when everything in the natural world is in perfect balance because the day and the night are the same length. The festival takes its name from Ostara or Ēostre, the goddess of renewal and rebirth, who has the head of a hare.

27th March *Passover*

Jewish people celebrate Passover to remember how the Prophet Moses helped the Israelites escape from Egypt to a new life in the Promised Land. They left in such a hurry that the dough for their bread had not risen, so that is why Jewish people eat matzo at Passover today – a flat bread which is 'unleavened'. This means it has no yeast in it and so does not rise like a normal loaf of bread.

29th March *Holi*

Holi is a Hindu festival also known as the 'festival of colours' or the 'festival of love', when Hindus celebrate the victory of good over evil and the arrival of spring. They meet to play and laugh, forget and forgive, and make up with people they have fallen out with!

Holi lasts for a night and a day, starting on the evening of the Purnima (full moon day). People light bonfires and pray that evil will be destroyed. Then they smear each other with coloured paints and drench each other using water pistols and water-filled balloons!

Recipe for *Matzo Pizza*

The thin, crispy bread that the Jews eat at Passover is delicious as a pizza base! If you don't want to make the *matzo*, you can buy them ready-made from most big supermarkets. They must be made quickly so that they do not rise at all because of the rules about eating unleavened bread during Passover.

You will need:

Greaseproof paper (optional)
Baking tray
Mixing bowl
Wooden spoon
Rolling pin
Fork

100 ml sunflower oil (plus extra for greasing)
250 g white flour plus some for dusting
½ teaspoon of sea salt
100 ml water

Vegetarian pizza toppings of your choice, e.g. tomato sauce, mini tomatoes, peppers, kosher cheese, kosher olives, herbs, spinach, mushrooms

1. Preheat the oven to 200°C/180°C fan/Gas Mark 6.
2. Oil the baking tray or line with greaseproof paper.
3. Mix the flour and salt in the bowl with the spoon. Add the oil and stir.
4. Add the water and knead the mixture with your hands until you have a soft dough. Add more water if it's too dry.
5. Sprinkle some flour on a work surface and tip the dough out, kneading it for about three minutes.
6. Flatten the dough with the rolling pin until it is about 5 mm thick and shape it to fit the baking tray.
7. Place the dough on the tray and prick it all over with the fork.
8. Cook for 2 minutes until the matzo base is crispy.
9. Take the matzo base out of the oven and ask an adult to help you to flip it, then cover it with the pizza toppings of your choice.
10. Put it back in the oven and cook until the toppings are cooked. This should take 5–10 minutes.

Make a *Mother's Day Promise Jar*

Mother's Day is a very old festival. People celebrated it in ancient Greece when the mother goddess, Rhea, was worshipped. Later, Christians celebrated the day as a time for people to go back to their 'mother' church if they had moved away from their home town. Nowadays, we spend the day saying thank you to our mothers or carers or special female relatives or friends with a card, gift or meal. What about making a promise jar to say thank you this Mother's Day?

You will need:

Scraps of paper – white or coloured
Scissors or pinking shears
Pen or pencil
Clean old jam jar – decorated with stickers or glitter glue pens if you like
Colourful recycled wrapping paper or pages from a magazine
Elastic band
Length of thin ribbon

TOP TIP
Why not make a lovely breakfast and lay the table – maybe with a vase of flowers, too? Then leave the jar of promises out as a surprise as well!

1. Cut your scraps of paper into squares that are about 6 cm x 6 cm, using the scissors or pinking shears.
2. Write a promise on each piece of paper. Ten is probably enough. Some ideas are: "I will make you a cup of tea." "I will walk the dog."
3. Fold each piece of paper in half and put them in the jar.
4. Put the lid, top down, on the sheet of wrapping paper or a page from a magazine and draw a larger circle around it. You can do this by hand – don't worry if it's not a perfect circle.
5. Cut out the large circle with the scissors or pinking shears.
6. Screw the lid on to the jar and place the large paper circle on top.
7. Fix it in place with the elastic band and tie some ribbon over the band.

WAKEY-WAKEY!

Creatures such as hedgehogs, dormice, bumblebees, butterflies and bats come out of hibernation at this time of year. They wake up from a long winter's sleep and immediately go searching for food to fill their empty bellies.

Maybe you have a tortoise as a pet? If so, you'll need to wake him or her up around this time. Wait until the outside temperature is at least 10°C before you move your tortoise outside, though. It will be a bit of a shock, moving from a cosy hibernation box to the chilly garden or patio!

OUT AND ABOUT

There are more birds and animals to see in March. Some of them, such as chiffchaffs and wheatears, are visitors from other countries. It will depend where you live in the UK as to whether you are likely to see these birds. Some of them are found only in wetland areas or by the sea.

CAN YOU SPOT...

| Chiffchaff | Sand martin | Sandwich tern | Blackcap |

| Chaffinch | Wheatear | Skylark | Lapwing |

DID YOU KNOW...

Skylarks start singing before the sun rises, so their voice is the first to be heard in the dawn chorus. Sadly, the numbers of skylarks are falling in all European countries. It is thought that this is because farmers now sow their crops in autumn rather than in spring – this means that skylarks no longer have the habitat they need in which to breed and survive.

HOW TO BUILD A NEST BOX

If you are going to make a nest box, you should complete it and hang it up early in March so that it is ready for the birds to start making their nest inside.

Nest boxes should always be made from wood. Metal and plastic are not good materials to use as they may mean that the nest will overheat or get wet and this will harm the eggs and the chicks. It is important that the inside of the box doesn't get too cold either.

You will need:

★ **Short planks of strong wood, at least 15 mm thick (oak or beech is best as pine is rather soft and doesn't last as long)**
★ **Saw**
★ **Stainless steel nails (not glue – nails allow water to drain out of the box)**
★ **Hammer**
★ **Waterproof hinge for the lid (see page 45)**
★ **Helpful grown-up!**

Follow the diagram below:

Make sure your grown-up drills a few holes in the base of your box so that any rain that does get in can drain out quickly.

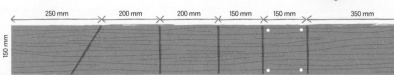

| 250 mm | 200 mm | 200 mm | 150 mm | 150 mm | 350 mm |

150 mm

1300 mm

TOP TIP

The number of swifts is falling. Encourage them to visit by building a larger nest box (55 mm hole) and attaching it to the side of your house or high up in a tree!

Hole sizes

Different birds need different-sized holes:

- **25 mm** or larger for blue, coal and marsh tit;

- **28 mm** or larger for great tit and tree sparrow;

- **32 mm** for house sparrow.

Making a hinge

A lid is important so that you can get into the box easily to check what is going on inside – and to clean it each season. Attach a waterproof hinge to the roof of the box, so that it can be lifted easily but won't fall off. You can use pieces of tyre inner tubes or cut-up plastic milk bottles to make your hinge. Cut the rubber or plastic to the width of the box, and then nail it along the back of the box and to the roof.

GET WET

Building a dam is a great outdoors activity now that spring is on its way. You'll need to ask an adult to help you find the best place to build your dam. And make sure everyone wears wellies and some waterproof clothing!

First choose a narrow stream of clean, shallow water where you can paddle safely. Then you need to start looking for driftwood, loose mud, rocks and pebbles. You'll use these to build the dam. You'll find the best bits and pieces at places where the stream bends, as rocks and things will tend to get stuck there.

See if you can stop the stream from flowing or change its direction by building up your dam. Where does the water go?

Don't forget to take down your dam before you go home so that the stream can flow freely again.

DID YOU KNOW...

Beavers create dams to make a pond of deep, quiet water where they like to build their homes or 'lodges'. The dams slow the flow of the water so that the beavers' homes do not get washed away.

DOWN BY THE RIVER

If you can get to a river, keep a sharp lookout for kingfishers. At this time of year the male bird is very busy, zipping along the surface of the water looking for fish – and a female to build a nest with!

CAN YOU SPOT...

TOP TIP
Note down what you find in your nature notebook!

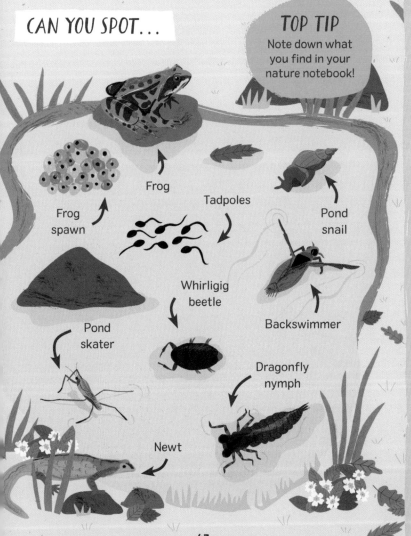

Frog

Frog spawn

Tadpoles

Pond snail

Whirligig beetle

Backswimmer

Pond skater

Dragonfly nymph

Newt

APRIL

SPECIAL DAYS

1st April Fool's Day

4th Easter Sunday (Christian celebration)

12th Ramadan begins (Muslim month of prayer and fasting)

22nd Earth Day

23rd St George's Day (England)/William Shakespeare's birthday

ANNIVERSARIES

95 years ago . . .

On 21 April 1926, Queen Elizabeth II was born. In 2015, she became the longest-reigning British monarch, having been on the throne since 1952. Before that, her great-great-grandmother Queen Victoria had reigned the longest.

400 years ago . . .

On 5 April 1621, the ship *The Mayflower* set out from Plymouth in Massachusetts, America, to return to Britain after leaving the first English settlers to start a new life in America.

> *"April hath put a spirit of youth in everything."*
>
> WILLIAM SHAKESPEARE (1564–1616)

A famous writer, T. S. Eliot, called April 'the cruellest month'. It's true that the weather can be very changeable but, thanks to those April showers, we start to see lots of signs of new life which signal that spring is well and truly on its way. Look out for beautiful blossom on the trees and green shoots in the flowerbeds.

April showers can be annoying. Those short, sharp bursts of rain seem to come from nowhere and disappear just as quickly. You have to remember to take an umbrella out with you in April even if the sun is shining when you leave the house! This is because the sky is full of cumulonimbus (those big, puffy white clouds) which burst into rain and then clear away again to leave blue sky.

It can still be very cold in the mornings, too – you might see frost on the grass early in the day. There can also be heavy snow in the hills. So basically, when you go out, be prepared for all weathers!

Phases of the Moon **in April 2021**

| **Last Quarter** | **New Moon** | **First Quarter** | **Full Moon** |
| 4th April | 12th April | 20th April | 27th April |

Do you know the difference between a new moon, a full moon and a blue moon?

A **new moon** is a moon we cannot see from Earth! This is because the moon is so close to the sun at this point, that the side facing us is in darkness. In other words, the moon is between the Earth and the sun and therefore is not lit up.

A **full moon** is when the complete circle of the moon can be seen in the sky. The full moon in April is called the 'Pink Moon'.

A **blue moon** happens when there are two full moons in the same month. The last blue moon was on 31 October 2020, and the next one will be 31 August 2023. This is because the moon goes through all of its phases in 28 days, whereas our months can be 28, 29, 30 or 31 days long. So every two or three years, there will be a month or two in the year when there are two full moons.

DID YOU KNOW...

On 23rd April, the Lyrids meteor shower will be at its height. You might be able to see shooting stars associated with the shower any time from 19th to 25th April if the night sky is clear.

CONSTELLATION OF THE MONTH

Hydra, the water snake, can be seen from January through to May, but it is at its highest point in the sky in April. It seems to suit the rainy month of April rather well to have a water snake as the constellation of the month!

The story behind Hydra comes from the Greek myths. One day the sun god, Apollo, sent a crow to fetch him a cup of water. When the mischievous crow came back, he gave Apollo a cup with a water snake in it instead! Apollo was so angry that he threw the snake and the crow into the sky and they became constellations of stars.

There is another Greek myth that has a monster in it called Hydra. This was a monster with many heads which the brave and strong hero Heracles had to kill.

FESTIVAL FUN

1st April *April Fool's Day*

April Fool's Day is celebrated by people playing tricks on one another. Sometimes there are even April Fool's Day stories on the news. One of the most famous of these was in 1957 on the BBC television programme *Panorama*. The programme reported that in Italy there were spaghetti trees! Lots of people believed this because in 1957 not many people in Britain had eaten spaghetti, so they didn't know that it was made from flour and water and it definitely did not grow on trees . . .

DID YOU KNOW...

There are a few unofficial rules about April Fool's Day tricks. The first is to do no harm – after all, the aim is to make someone look and feel silly. The second is that you can only play tricks before midday. If you try to trick someone in the afternoon, you become the fool!

12th April *Ramadan Begins*

The month of Ramadan traditionally begins after the new moon, so the date for Ramadan changes from year to year. During Ramadan, Muslims hold a fast during the hours of daylight, which means they are not allowed to eat or drink from the moment the sun comes up until the moment it sets. People must also try not to gossip or fight during Ramadan. Muslims use the daylight hours to focus on saying prayers and giving money and possessions to charity. Some people try to learn the whole holy book, the *Qur'an*, during this time!

FESTIVAL FUN

4th April *Easter Sunday*

The Christian festival of Easter starts on the Thursday before Easter Sunday with a day called 'Maundy Thursday', when Christians believe that Jesus invited his followers to a meal called the 'Last Supper'. Easter ends on Easter Sunday, when Christians believe that Jesus came back from the dead. It is a time for new life and rebirth. Easter eggs are also popular on this day.

Some people believe that the tradition for giving and receiving Easter eggs comes from the pagan festival Ostara, or Ēostre. The Easter Bunny, who is supposed to bring the eggs, is thought to come from the pagan religion, which has the Hare as the symbol of new life. Christians use the symbol of the Easter egg to represent rebirth and the resurrection of Jesus. Since the 13th century, Christians have celebrated the end of Lent and beginning of Easter by decorating and painting eggs.

EGG–CELLENT ACTIVITIES

Today, a lot of people in Britain give and receive Easter eggs over Easter weekend, whether or not they celebrate any religious festivals.

The Hunt is On!

Easter egg hunts are always exciting. You could ask an adult to hide mini chocolate eggs outside in the garden or in an area of your local park, or even while you are out on a walk. Then see how quickly you can find them – and don't eat too many on the way!

If the April showers are stopping you from going outside, why not have your Easter egg hunt in your home? There are plenty of places to hide eggs indoors. Make sure you find them all though – there's nothing worse than sitting on a forgotten Easter egg that someone has hidden under a cushion!

Decorating *Eggs*

You will need:

Hard-boiled eggs (cooled)
Wax crayons
White vinegar
Food colouring
Hot water
Different bowl for each colour dye
Tablespoon
Kitchen paper

1. *Draw a simple design on the egg with a wax crayon.*
2. *Make dye by mixing 1 tablespoon of vinegar with 1 tablespoon of food colouring in a small bowl and adding ¾ cup of hot water.*
3. *Place a hard-boiled egg on a spoon and lower it gently into the bowl.*
4. *Leave the egg in the dye for a few minutes.*
5. *Lift out the egg and place it carefully on a piece of kitchen paper.*
6. *As the egg dries, the pattern you drew will appear through the dye!*

BE GREEN FOR EARTH DAY

22nd April is Earth Day. This is a day to focus on what we can do to help the environment and protect our planet. The first Earth Day was in 1970. It was set up by an American politician called Senator Gaylord Nelson because he thought it was important for children to be taught about the environment in school.

Here are some things you could do on Earth Day:

★ Walk or cycle to school instead of going by car or bus.
★ Turn off lights when you leave the room.
★ Turn off electrical appliances such as the TV, chargers and computer at the wall when you are not using them.
★ Try not to use a computer, tablet or the TV at all for just one day!
★ Get outside and find a green space to walk or play in – you don't have to have a garden or live in the country to do this. Find a square or a park and take time to look at the trees, plants, birds and insects.
★ If you have space at home, why not do some spring planting?
★ Ask your grown-ups if you can swap from chemical cleaning products to more environmentally friendly options. Did you know that you can do a lot of cleaning using natural things such as vinegar water and lemon juice?
★ Remember to take a cloth bag or a 'bag for life' when you go shopping to avoid using a plastic bag.
★ Did you know that meat production uses much more energy than plants? Try eating vegetarian food for one day. There are lots of delicious recipes to try – some are in this book!
★ Take a refillable drink bottle out with you instead of buying water or juice in plastic bottles.

HOW DOES YOUR GARDEN GROW?

Once the weather warms up, April is a great time to start planting things. You don't need a big garden – in fact, you don't need a garden at all. A lot of flowers, fruits and vegetables can be planted in pots and grown on a windowsill or patio area.

Here are some easy plants to grow:

Geraniums   Lavender   Dahlia   Strawberries

Here are some plants you can grow from seed:

Runner beans   Sweet peas   Nasturtiums   Radishes

Carrots   Sunflowers   Watercress

TOP TIP
Don't forget to water your plants once a day.

Make an *Egghead*

This is a fun indoor gardening activity – and you can eat the results! Use the larger part of any egg shells saved from after you've had boiled eggs or after you've used some eggs for baking.

You will need:

Empty eggshells
Empty egg box
Felt-tip pens
Cotton wool
Cress seeds

TOP TIP
If you don't want to make edible eggheads, you can use grass seed instead of cress. The grass will grow back so you can style your eggheads' hair again and again.

1. Wash out the eggshells and sit them in the egg box.
2. Draw on some crazy faces with the felt-tip pens.
3. Put some cotton wool inside the shells and sprinkle some water on to make it damp.
4. Sprinkle lots of cress seeds all over the wet cotton wool – the more seeds you pour in, the more 'hair' your eggheads will grow!
5. Put the box of eggheads on a sunny windowsill and wait for the 'hair' to sprout.
6. Check the cotton wool each day and add a little water if the cotton wool feels dry when you touch it. Do not over-water the cress.
7. When the cress 'hair' has grown, you can give your eggheads a haircut! Use scissors to cut the cress and add it to chopped-up boiled eggs and mayonnaise for a tasty sandwich filling.
8. When you're finished with your eggheads, you can put them in the compost.

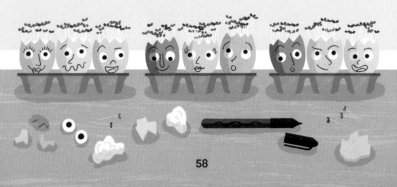

EAT YOUR GREENS!

Purple sprouting broccoli is in the shops and markets at this time of year. It's not only very tasty, it is packed full of vitamins and iron, so it's very good for you too. You can eat it boiled or steamed, or you can roast it with olive oil. It is also very good dipped in boiled eggs instead of toast soldiers. Here's a yummy pasta recipe for you to try.

Recipe for *Purple Sprouting Broccoli Pasta*

You will need:

Tablespoon
Frying pan
2 large saucepans
Steamer (optional)
Food blender
Wooden spoon
Colander
Grater

1 garlic clove, chopped or pressed
Olive oil
350 g penne or farfalle pasta
400 g purple sprouting broccoli, trimmed
Black pepper
Parmesan cheese, grated

1. Put the garlic and a tablespoon of olive oil into the frying pan.
2. Cook the garlic for a couple of minutes, but do not let it burn, then remove the pan from the heat.
3. Cook the pasta in boiling water in one of the saucepans, following the directions on the packet.
4. Boil the broccoli in another saucepan for about three minutes or, if you have a steamer, steam it above the pasta for about five minutes until the stems are soft.
5. Take half of the broccoli and blend it until you have a puree. Cut the remaining broccoli into chunks and toss it into the pan. Add a little olive oil and black pepper if you like.

6. Drain the pasta and stir the broccoli puree into it. Serve with lots of grated parmesan. Delicious and healthy!

PARK LIFE

There's lots going on in local parks now that the days are longer and lighter. Why not join a park run? You don't have to be a fast runner, so you can chat as you run if you like! And there's often a park café nearby where you can go afterwards to have a well-earned snack and drink.

Look at the website **www.parkrun.org.uk** to find out where your nearest junior park run is. You will need to ask an adult to help you register online before you join a park run.

If running is not for you, take a scooter, skateboard or bike to the park. Or ask an adult if you can volunteer to walk a dog from your local dogs' home if there is one near you. (Or walk your own dog, of course!)

Whatever you choose to do, getting outside and breathing in the spring air will make you smile.

BIRDS ON THE MOVE

The birds are getting noisier now! You might find that you are woken up earlier by the sound of a wood pigeon cooing loudly outside your window. Then other smaller birds join in with their different sounds. This is called the 'dawn chorus'. If you've got time in the morning, it's lovely to lie in bed and just listen to the music the birds make – it's like having a free concert right outside your window!

More and more birds are finding their way back to Britain after the winter. Look out for the first swallows, swifts and house martins later in the month.

Swallow

Swift

House martin

The bird that people think of most in April is the cuckoo. It spends the winter in Africa but comes back to Britain during this month.

Cuckoo

DID YOU KNOW...

★ It is traditional for people to write to *The Times* newspaper when they hear the first cuckoo of spring!

★ Each spring a female will lay between 12 and 22 eggs, all in other birds' nests.

★ A female cuckoo will lay her eggs in a nest belonging to the same kind of bird that looked after her when she was a chick.

★ Adult cuckoos move back to Africa as soon as their chicks are hatched. This can be as early as the end of June.

★ Young cuckoos follow their parents back to Africa several weeks later.

MAY

SPECIAL DAYS

1st Beltane (pagan celebration)/May Day

3rd Early May bank holiday

13th Eid al-Fitr (end of Ramadan)/
Ascension Day

17th Shavuot (Jewish festival of weeks)

23rd Whitsun/Pentecost (Christian
celebration)

31st Spring bank holiday

ANNIVERSARIES

70 years ago . . .

On 3 May 1951, the Royal Festival Hall was opened in London on the South Bank of the River Thames. It was built as part of the celebrations for the Festival of Britain, which was created to give people hope after the Second World War.

225 years ago . . .

On 14 May 1796, Sir Edward Jenner tested the first ever vaccine. He gave his gardener's son a small amount of cowpox to see if it stopped him from getting the full disease. It worked, and he went on to invent the smallpox vaccination we still use today.

> *"A swarm of bees in May*
> *Is worth a load of hay."*

Hedgerows are at their most beautiful in May. They are full of wildflowers which attract lots of insects and butterflies. The traditional saying above gives us a good picture of what is going on in nature in May. It is a very busy month for bees! They are working hard to gather nectar to feed on, and while they do this, they are also helping plants to grow through 'pollination'. So lots of busy bees in May means plenty of yummy bread, cereal, fruit and vegetables for us. It's a good idea to plant wildflowers in your garden or allotment if you can as this will feed the bees.

At the beginning of the month there is also an explosion of golden dandelions everywhere. Birds such as goldfinches love the seeds: you'll see lots of these beautiful birds flocking to nibble the seeds just before the flowers turn into dandelion 'clocks'.

DID YOU KNOW...

The word 'dandelion' comes from the French, '*dents de lion*' which means 'lion's teeth', but the French actually call them *pissenlit* which means 'wet the bed', because eating the leaves makes you wee a lot!

Why is May Called May?

Nobody knows for sure, but it seems likely that this month was named after the Greek goddess Maia, who was goddess of fertility. Her festival is still celebrated by some people on 15th May.

May Birth Signs

Taurus The sign of the bull. Some people believe that anyone with a birthday which falls between 20th April and 21st May was born under this sign. They are supposed to be sensible and good at making and fixing things.

Gemini The sign of the twins. Anyone born between 21st May and 21st June is a Gemini. They are supposed to be very chatty!

Meteor Shower *Eta Aquariids*

These meteors usually fall sometime between 19th April and 28th May. This year, you should be able to see the shower from the night of 6th May to the morning of 7th May. About 30 meteors will fall each hour. The shower is formed by particles of dust left behind by Halley's Comet. This comet has been known about since ancient times and is the only comet that can be seen from Earth without using a telescope.

If you want to see the meteor shower, you will have to stay up late or get up very early! The best spot to see it from will be a very dark place from about midnight. The meteors can appear anywhere in the sky.

65

FESTIVAL FUN

1st May *Beltane*

The old Gaelic word *Beltane* means 'bright fire'. This ancient pagan festival celebrates the return of summer and is also known as the 'Feast of the Good Fires'. It marks the time of year halfway between the spring equinox and the summer solstice.

Long ago, it was a time when farmers let their cows and sheep back out into the fields after the cold weather. To make sure that their animals would stay healthy, the farmers would light big bonfires and burn special herbs on them. They would then make their animals walk in between the fires so that they could breathe in the purifying smells. This was supposed to protect them from illness.

1st May *May Day*

May Day celebrations are often mixed in with Beltane bonfires. A May queen is chosen and either two people carry her, or she rides through the streets on a cart pulled by a horse. The cart is covered in flowers and the May queen wears flowers in her hair. She sometimes has a man or boy with her representing the Green Man, who is the pagan god of nature. People dance around a maypole, which is a long stick with coloured ribbons coming from the top. Each person takes a ribbon and dances around the pole, weaving in and out of each other until the pole is tightly wrapped in the ribbons. This is done to symbolise how the growing strength of the sun is finding its way into the land. Traditionally, May Day was a time for weddings and lots of parties.

13th May *Eid al-Fitr*

Eid al-Fitr is an Islamic festival that is celebrated by Muslims all over the world. It is the day which ends Ramadan and it falls on or near the date of a new moon. During Eid, Muslim people celebrate with delicious food, by praying and by giving money to charity.

13th May *Ascension Day*

Ascension Day is a Christian festival and is a very important date in the Christian calendar. The word 'ascension' means 'rising up'. According to the Bible, 40 days after Easter Sunday Jesus ascended, or rose up, to heaven and went to sit at the right-hand side of God. Ascension Day is always celebrated on a Thursday. However, not all countries hold the feast on this day. In Germany, Father's Day is celebrated on the same day.

17th May *Shavuot*

Shavuot is a Jewish festival during which Jewish people remember the day that God gave the Prophet Moses the holy scriptures, the *Torah*. All Jewish people go to the synagogue on the first day of Shavuot to hear the reading of the Ten Commandments. This is a list of laws for living a good life. They can be found in the *Torah*, the *Qur'an* and in the *Bible*, too.

23rd May *Pentecost or Whitsun*

Pentecost or Whitsun is the 8th Sunday after Easter. On this day, Christians remember that God sent the Holy Spirit to be with the followers of Jesus. In Britain the festival borrowed some of the ideas from the May festival of Beltane, making it yet another celebration of summer arriving. In the north-west of England some churches and chapels still hold 'Whit walks' – parades that include brass bands, choirs and girls dressed in white.

Make an *Eid Mobile*

During the celebrations for Eid-al-Fitr many Muslims decorate their houses. This mobile is a lovely decoration to have in the house and is very easy to make. The crescent moon and star are on the flags of many Islamic countries, but they are not the symbols of the religion of Islam. The moon is important, however, as the Islamic calendar follows the cycle of the moon. This is why festivals such as Eid fall on different dates in the calendar that is more widely used in Britain.

You will need:

Card
Scissors
Silver, gold or white paint, or stickers
String or wool
Twig or wooden lolly stick

1. *Draw a crescent moon and star on your card and carefully cut them out.*
2. *Decorate or paint both side of each shape with paint or stickers.*
3. *Ask an adult to help you punch a hole in the top of each shape.*
4. *Thread a piece of string or wool through each hole.*
5. *Tie the other ends of the string or wool to the twig or lolly stick.*
6. *Tie a piece of string to the middle of the twig or lolly stick so you can hang your mobile up.*
7. *Pin the mobile up in your room!*

COUNTRYSIDE CODE

Did you know that there are rules you should follow when you are out walking in the countryside? They are designed to make the countryside safe for everyone so that we can all enjoy it.

1 Respect the local community
Farmers work hard all year round to grow the food we eat and to look after their animals. If you see a farm animal, remember it is not a pet. Do not feed or stroke it. And if you are in a car or on a bike, make sure you slow down for farm animals so you don't frighten them.

2 Leave gates as you find them
If you walk up to a gate and it is closed, make sure you close it behind you. The farmer probably wants to keep the animals from running away. However, if you find a gate open, do not close it behind you as a farmer might be moving animals from one field to the next.

3 Stick to paths and follow signs
Some land is open to everyone to walk on, but some is private. If you are not sure, check a detailed map and follow the signs. This is for your own safety as well as to respect people's privacy and to help look after important habitats. You wouldn't want to walk into a field with an angry bull in it, or a pair of ground-nesting lapwings!

4 Leave no trace

Always take your litter away with you. Many places in the countryside do not have public bins but this doesn't mean you can drop your rubbish on the ground. Litter is dangerous to wildlife and farm animals as they can hurt themselves on it or end up eating it which could make them seriously ill.

5 Look after your dog

It is important to keep dogs under control in case they run into a field of farm animals and scare them. Look out for signs asking you to keep your dog on the lead. If you have to walk through a field of cows, your dog should be on a lead, but if you are approached by the cows, it would be better to let your dog off their lead. The dog will be safer and so will you. Always remember to pick up any mess your dog makes, too, and carry it to the nearest dog bin, as this can make farm animals sick!

BABY WILD ANIMAL SPOTTING

There are so many more animals around in May – many of them are babies. May is the perfect time for spotting young fox cubs or badgers. If you have ever watched *Springwatch* on the BBC, you will have seen how active these animals are, particularly at night.

A simple way to try spotting wildlife at night is to dress in dark clothing and sit very quietly in the garden while the sun goes down. Foxes, badgers, hedgehogs and bats become more active in the early evening. They come out of their homes looking for slugs, worms and insects to eat. Now that the weather is warmer, there is a lot more food around!

Hedgehogs

These lovely little animals are sadly becoming very rare. There are now fewer than half the number of hedgehogs in the wild as there were in the year 2000. This is possibly because there are fewer hedges for them to live in as so many hedgerows have been replaced with fences. The other problem is traffic. Many hedgehogs are killed on the roads. Some towns have special 'Hedgehog Crossing' signs to warn drivers to go slowly and look out for the creatures.

If you would like to get a hedgehog sign to put up where you live, visit **www.britishhedgehogs.org.uk**

TOP TIP
Tinned cat food is a favourite treat for badgers, foxes and hedgehogs.

TAKE ME TO THE RIVER

One of the most relaxing things you can do on a sunny day in May is to get out in a boat! There are many places all over Britain where you can hire kayaks, canoes, rowing boats or paddle boards. It is the best way to see river wildlife as you are usually moving slowly and quietly and you are at the same level as many of the animals, birds and insects. If you spot something up ahead, stop paddling and float slowly and quietly towards what you want to observe. It's a good idea to bring binoculars with you. If you are worried about dropping things in the water, you can hire or buy waterproof bags which float!

This is a perfect time of year for spotting brown trout which rise to the surface to eat the hatching mayflies. There will also be lots of little ducklings, cygnets, goslings and chicks around. Moorhen chicks have extremely fluffy black bodies with incredibly long legs and huge feet! You should also look out for kingfishers which will be hunting a lot at this time of year, catching fish, of course, but also tadpoles and damselflies.

Build a *Bug Hotel*

Insects and spiders are gardeners' friends! Encouraging small creatures such as bees, beetles and woodlice into your garden at home or school will help the plants to grow – so you'll be doing everyone a favour if you build a lovely shelter for the minibeasts outside.

You will need:

Bricks with holes in
Planks of wood
Dead wood
Bark
Hollow bamboo canes
Dead hollow stems from plants
Straw
Moss
Dry leaves
Woodchips
Old terracotta plant pots
Old roof tiles
Pine cones
Sand
Soil
Roofing felt

1 *Choose the spot where you want your hotel to be. Damp places are best for most bugs, but if you want to attract bees you'll need a sunnier spot.*

2 *Put some bricks on the ground to make a strong base, leaving some gaps between them – an H-shape is best.*

3 *Lay planks of wood across the bricks to make a 'floor'.*

4 *Cover the planks with dead wood and bark – beetles, centipedes and woodlice will love this. Spiders, too!*

5 *Put some more bricks on the edges of the 'floor' to add another level and lay more planks of wood across them.*

6 *Pack this next level with bamboo or other hollow stems for insects to crawl into.*

7 *Keep adding layers filled with other materials until you have the kind of hotel you want.*

8 *To add a roof, you can nail roofing felt on to the last area of wood – ask an adult to help.*

TOP TIP
Larger holes
made from broken
flowerpots or tiles are
wonderful homes for
toads and frogs.

JUNE

SPECIAL DAYS

5th World Environment Day

12th The Queen's official birthday/
Trooping the Colour (the Queen's
birthday parade)

20th Father's Day

21st Summer solstice

24th Midsummer's Day

ANNIVERSARIES

95 years ago . . .

On 1 June 1926, Marilyn Monroe was born. She was a beautiful American actor, model and singer and was also the inspiration for some famous prints made by the American artist Andy Warhol.

100 years ago . . .

On 10 June 1921, the Duke of Edinburgh, Prince Phillip, was born.

190 years ago . . .

On 1 June 1831, James Clark Ross discovered the Magnetic North Pole. This is where a compass points to when it is pointing north because it follows the magnetic fields to this spot. It is not the same as the place called the North Pole, which is the most northerly point on the globe.

> *"At midnight, in the month of June,*
> *I stand beneath the mystic moon."*

EDGAR ALLAN POE (1809–1849)

Summertime is here at last! It's time for strawberries and cream and barbecues. The roses are out in the gardens and parks and, of course, there are lots of long, hot, sunny days to look forward to – right? Well . . . there will be some sunshine, but often we get excited and plan summer outdoor activities in Britain, only to find that the rain means we have to change our plans.

Nevertheless, this is the month to enjoy long days outside. When you get home from school it feels as though you have so much extra time to have fun! You can meet your friends in the park for football or just laze around chatting in the shade eating ice cream. June has the longest day

DID YOU KNOW...

No month ever begins on the same day of the week as the month of June.

of the year, so by 21st June you won't see the sun go down until around 10 p.m. The full moon occurs at midsummer, so you'll have to stay up late if you want to see it!

78

Why is June Called June?

The month of June was probably named after the Roman god Juno. She was the wife of Jupiter, who was the king of the gods. Juno was the goddess of marriage. Some people think it is good luck to get married in June. The Anglo-Saxons called it *Sera Monath*, which means 'dry month'. (Maybe it didn't rain so much back then!)

Phases of the Moon **in June 2021**

Last Quarter	**New Moon**	**First Quarter**	**Full Moon**
2nd June	10th June	18th June	24th June

Constellation of the Month

Cassiopeia was a vain queen in Greek mythology. The legend tells us that she was thrown into the sky as a constellation after enraging Poseidon, the god of the sea. She boasted to him that her daughter, Andromeda, was more beautiful than his sea nymphs. She should have known that it is never a good idea to make an ancient god angry!

FESTIVAL FUN

12th June *The Queen's Official Birthday*

This is always celebrated on the second Saturday in June. The Queen appears on the balcony of Buckingham Palace in London to watch the Trooping of the Colour. The soldiers wear special uniforms to show which regiment they belong to. Music is played by the Foot Guards' Band and the Band of the Household Cavalry, who are on horseback. There are 400 musicians in total!

The Queen gives awards called 'Birthday Honours' to people who have done something special in their lives, such as helping people in their community or charity work.

Birthstone and Birth Flower

If your birthday is in June, your birthstone can be either pearl or moonstone. Both are supposed to bring health and long life. The official flower of June is the honeysuckle. Bees, butterflies and birds love this sweet-smelling plant.

20th June *Father's Day*

Father's Day is a day to remember dads, and also grandfathers or other male relatives or carers who are special people in our lives. The day always falls on the third Sunday in June. Many people celebrate by making cards or giving their male relative or carer a treat to show how much they are loved. You could plan a camping trip together for a night. You don't have to go anywhere special – you could just camp in the garden. Or if it's raining, choose your favourite film to watch together and make some popcorn to enjoy.

21ˢᵗ JUNE SUMMER SOLSTICE

"In winter I get up at night
and dress by yellow candle-light.
In summer, quite the other way,
I have to go to bed by day."

ROBERT LOUIS STEVENSON (1850–1894)

It can be very annoying when you have to go to bed when the sun is still up! It is particularly hard to go to sleep on the longest day of the year. Pagans traditionally do not go to bed at all on this night! They stay up to welcome the sunrise and give thanks for its power and warmth.

One famous pagan summer solstice celebration happens at Stonehenge, a circle of standing stones in Salisbury in the west of England. People meet at the stones to watch the sunrise at about 4.45 a.m. This is an act of worship and there is a lot of music and dancing.

The summer solstice is also known as *Litha*, which is an Anglo-Saxon word for 'midsummer'. Bonfires were lit on the tops of hills – some places in Britain still do this. The bonfire represents the strength, light and heat of the sun. Young men used to leap over them for luck!

Morris Dancing

Morris dancing is a form of English folk dance with music. The dancers wear bell pads on their legs to add to the music and they use sticks and handkerchiefs. The sticks are clashed together in a pretend sword fight. The handkerchiefs are used to make the dance flow as the dancers wave them in the air. They wear white clothing with colourful ribbons and sometimes brightly coloured jackets as well. Music is played on accordions, concertinas, violins, flutes, tambourines and drums. Dances have names such as 'Cuckoo's Nest', 'Bean Setting', 'Bonny Green' and 'Hunt the Squirrel'!

DID YOU KNOW...

In the southern hemisphere, the summer solstice is actually the winter solstice! So people living in places south of the equator have the shortest day of the year while people in Britain enjoy the longest day.

DON'T BE A GOOSEBERRY!

Gooseberries are funny little hard, hairy green fruit that don't look very attractive, and they grow on very spiky bushes, so you have to be careful and wear gardening gloves if you want to pick any yourself. They are ripe late in June and go on being edible into early July, depending where you are in the country. You can, of course, also find them in the shops around this time – without the spikes!

There are a few myths and sayings surrounding the poor old gooseberry. "Don't be a gooseberry," means "Don't be left out – join in the fun!" This may be because of the green and spiky appearance of the fruit which makes us think of someone who isn't friendly. Gooseberries used also to be known as fayberries because of the ancient belief that fairies used to hide in gooseberry bushes if they were frightened.

They may not look very nice raw, but gooseberries are delicious when stewed with sugar or used in cakes and jams and tarts. They are also a good source of vitamin C.

Recipe for *Gooseberry Tart*

Here is a yummy tart for you to try. It is very easy to make and delicious served with vanilla ice cream or natural yoghurt.

You will need:

Rolling pin
23 cm loose-bottomed tart tin
Blunt knife
Greaseproof paper
Baking beans or dried peas or lentils
Wire rack
Whisk
Mixing bowl

250 g ready-made shortcrust pastry
Plain flour for dusting
2 large eggs
200 ml double cream
85 g caster sugar
1 teaspoon of vanilla extract
300 g gooseberries, topped and tailed
Icing sugar to serve (optional)

1. *Roll out the pastry on a lightly floured surface until it is large enough to line the tin.*
2. *Use the knife to trim off any pastry that is hanging over the edge.*
3. *Line the pastry with greaseproof paper. Fill it with the baking beans or peas or lentils. Put it in the fridge for 30 minutes.*
4. *Meanwhile, heat the oven to 200°C/180°C fan/Gas Mark 6.*
5. *After the pastry has chilled, bake it for 15 minutes.*
6. *Carefully lift out the greaseproof paper and beans and put to one side.*
7. *Bake the pastry for five more minutes until it looks golden, like a biscuit. Put to one side on the wire rack to cool slightly.*
8. *Whisk together the eggs, cream, sugar and vanilla extract in the bowl.*
9. *Scatter the gooseberries on top of the cooked pastry.*
10. *Pour the vanilla mixture over the berries.*
11. *Put the whole thing back in the oven and bake for 35–40 minutes.*
12. *The vanilla mixture should now be set.*
13. *Cool a little on the wire rack before serving.*
14. *If you prefer, you can eat the tart cold, dusted with icing sugar.*

BUTTERFLIES AND CATERPILLARS

We're Going on a Caterpillar Hunt!

Caterpillars are among the most fascinating of small creatures. They eat so much and grow so fast! And then, before you know it, they have turned into beautiful butterflies.

You will need:

Jar or small pot
Cling film with holes in
Magnifying glass or
minibeast pot

How to find caterpillars:

1. *Look for holes in leaves and missing parts of plants. Caterpillars spend every moment of every day munching their way through leaf after leaf. Sometimes the holes are as big as your fingernail, sometimes they are tiny pinpricks – it depends on the size of the caterpillar.*

2. *Can you find any little black blobs on the leaves? These are caterpillar poo. The proper name for them is 'frass'. If you see any, you'll know a caterpillar is nearby.*

3. *What about any tiny glassy green balls? These are butterfly or moth eggs, which means small caterpillars will soon be hatching.*

4. *Sometimes you might see strands of silk on a plant. It's not only spiders who spin silk, so do some caterpillars. They use them to make trails to walk around on or to make cocoons.*

When you find caterpillars, you can gently tip them into your pot to observe them. Don't forget to put some of the leaves you found them on into the pot so that your hungry caterpillars don't get even hungrier! Remember to return the caterpillars where you found them, so that they can turn into beautiful butterflies.

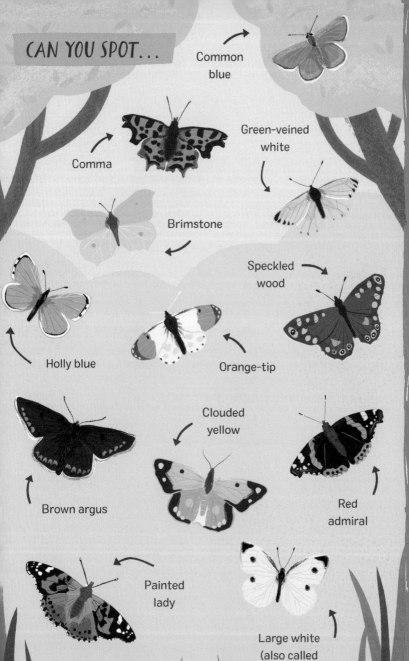

CAN YOU SPOT...

Common
blue

Comma

Green-veined
white

Brimstone

Speckled
wood

Holly blue

Orange-tip

Clouded
yellow

Brown argus

Red
admiral

Painted
lady

Large white
(also called
cabbage white)

87

CARRY ON CAMPING

There is something very exciting about setting up camp in the summer, even if it's just in your own garden or in a park or field near your home. But it's not so exciting when the British summer lets us down by chucking rain on our tents!

If you are having a wet and miserable June this year, why not set up camp indoors? Ask an adult first, of course. In fact, you'll probably need an adult to help with this activity.

The best tent to use is a pop-up tent – the kind that you might take to the beach, for example – as these do not need tent pegs. If you don't have one of these, ask if you can use big cushions and blankets or a table and blankets to make your own 'tent' or den.

You can do this in any room where there is space. It's more fun if you don't do it in the room you normally sleep in, as that makes it feel more like camping!

RAINY DAY FUN

There's nothing worse than a rainy day in the summer, is there? Well, maybe after trying one of these activities, you'll change your mind!

★ Ask for any cardboard boxes which are in the recycling pile and use them to build a town in the sitting room!

★ Put on a play or a show for your family. You could ask for some old socks to make puppets out of.

★ How about making a family magazine? Interview your family about their lives then write about them. Ask for old photos you can cut up and glue into the magazine.

★ Make cupcakes and decorate them – and then eat them. You deserve a treat on a day like this!

★ Go to the library and get ready for the Summer Reading Challenge, which starts next month. You need to choose six books to read over the summer so that you can collect all your stickers from the library.

JULY

SPECIAL DAYS

11th Sea Sunday (Christian celebration)

12th Battle of the Boyne
(Northern Ireland)

15th St Swithun's Day

20th Eid al-Adha (Muslim celebration)

25th St James's Day (Grotto Day)

ANNIVERSARIES

25 years ago . . .

On 5 July 1996, Dolly the sheep was born. She was the first mammal to be cloned from a somatic cell, which means that she was created as an identical copy of another sheep using a cell from the sheep's body.

75 years ago . . .

On 5 July 1946, the first bikini was shown at a fashion show in Paris.

200 years ago . . .

On 19 July 1821, it was the coronation of King George IV, King of Great Britain and Ireland.

> *"In scorched July*
> *The storm-clouds fly."*

CHRISTINA ROSSETTI (1830–1894)

At last the school holidays are here – weeks and weeks of free time to do whatever you like! It would be wonderful if we could rely on the weather to be fine for the whole of the holidays, but July can be a particularly stormy month. In fact, you are more likely to experience a thunderstorm during this month than at any other time during the year. This is because storms develop when there is a layer of warm air near the ground underneath a layer of much colder air. This is much more common in the summer when the days are longer, as there is more sunshine and therefore more energy.

But don't worry – there will still be golden days when you can rush to the beach or have long, lazy picnics in the park. And when the weather does break, just pull on some waterproof clothes and go out to splash in the puddles and breathe in the lovely smell of summer rain!

Why is July Called July?

It was named to honour the Roman statesman Julius Caesar as it was the month in which he was born (12th July). Before that, it was known as *Quintilis* – Latin for 'fifth' – as this was the fifth month in the Roman year before the calendar was changed. The Anglo-Saxons called it *Heymonath* as this is haymaking time.

 Phases of the Moon **in July 2021**

Last Quarter	**New Moon**	**First Quarter**	**Full Moon**
1st July	10th July	17th July	24th July

The full moon this month is known as the Buck Moon. Another name is the Thunder Moon because of the fact that there are often storms in the summer. Anglo-Saxons called it the Hay Moon because of haymaking or Wort Moon as it's the time to gather herbs (or worts) for using as spices and medicine.

DID YOU KNOW...

The Buck Moon gets its name from the new antlers that grow every summer from a buck (male) deer's forehead.

WHATEVER THE WEATHER

15th July *St Swithun's Day*

On St Swithun's Day there is a saying:

> *"St Swithun's Day, if thou dost rain,*
> *for forty days it will remain.*
> *St Swithun's Day, if thou be fair,*
> *for forty days 'twill rain nae mair."*

Thankfully, this is rarely true! St Swithun was the Bishop of Winchester. When he died in 862 CE, he was buried in front of the west door of the old Saxon cathedral building because he had said he wanted to be buried outdoors. He lay there for over 100 years. When another bishop came along in 971 CE, he wanted to have a new patron saint, so he dug up poor old St Swithun on his feast day, 15th July, and moved him to a tomb inside! That day there was a terrible storm which lasted for 40 days and 40 nights. Many people believed that this happened because the saint was not happy about being moved indoors, so that is where the saying about the weather comes from.

DID YOU KNOW...

The phrase 'the dog days of summer' comes from Roman times. It has more to do with stars than dogs! Towards the end of July, Sirius (known as the 'Dog Star') begins to rise in the sky just before the sun. It is so bright that the Romans believed it gave extra heat to the sun and was responsible for hot days in summer.

FESTIVAL FUN

20th July *Eid al-Adha*

This is an Islamic festival that marks the end of the *hajj* pilgrimage to the holy city of Mecca. It commemorates how Ibrahim was willing to sacrifice his son Isma'il to God. Allah stopped the sacrifice and gave Ibrahim a lamb to kill instead. A version of this story is also found in the Jewish *Torah* and the Old Testament of the Christian *Bible*.

Many Muslims wear new clothes or their nicest outfits for this festival and attend a prayer service at a mosque. They also send Eid cards to family and friends, give money to charity, and give each other gifts.

25th July *St James's Day or Grotto Day*

There is an old tradition that on St James's Day, children would make 'grottoes' or little caves out of seashells. This is because the scallop shell is supposed to be the symbol for St James who was one of the followers of Jesus.

Whitstable Oyster Festival begins on St James's Day. An old Kentish tradition says that Julius Caesar went to Britain because he loved the Whitstable oysters! The festival is a celebration of thanksgiving that still survives today.

Make a *Seashell Grotto*

If you go to the seaside this month, you'll be sure to collect some shells from the beach. Why not make your own St James's grotto by the sea? Make a sandcastle and then decorate it with as many different kinds of shells and pebbles as you can find.

SEASIDE COLLECTOR'S GUIDE

Cockle

Auger shell

Banded wedge shell

Common limpet

Oyster   Crab shell

Common mussel   Dog whelk

Periwinkle

Razor shell

Shark's tooth

Slipper limpet

Sea potato

HUG A TREE!

When you are out walking this month, take time to look at the trees you find. They will be in full leaf now, and will provide you with lots of cooling shade if you are walking on a hot day. Trees are very important for our environment. They are the biggest plants on the planet, and produce lots of oxygen for us to breathe. They also store carbon, make the soil rich and give life and a home to the world's wildlife. So give a tree a hug today and say thank you! They do a lot for us.

Ash

Silver birch

Oak

Beech

Sycamore

Horse chestnut

BARKING MAD FUN

This is the sort of activity you can do on a drizzly day as the branches and leaves will shelter you from a light shower. You can do it on a hot day too, of course, as the branches and leaves will provide you with shade! Take a few sheets of paper and some crayons out into the woods or garden or out into your local park and have fun creating some beautiful colourful patterns. You could then use the paper as wrapping paper, make greetings cards from it or frame your lovely pattern with some twigs and give it as a gift.

You will need:

Tree – or 2 or 3!
Plain paper
Wax crayons

Avoid this activity on windy days.

1 Choose an interesting tree. The big old knobbly ones are the best, because the patterns in their bark are bigger.

2 Press the paper against the bark and hold it in place. You might need to ask a grown-up to help you keep it steady.

3 Press your crayon sideways firmly against the paper and rub until the pattern starts to come through. Try not to press too hard, or you'll rip the paper.

4 When the pattern has come through, remove the paper.

99

OUT IN THE GARDEN

There are lots of jobs to do now that the weather is warmer. The most important job you can help with is watering the plants if there hasn't been enough rain. It is always best to do the watering in the evening because if the day gets hot, the water can evaporate too quickly and the poor plants can get burnt. Tomato plants and runner beans need a lot of water at this time of year. So do any flowers you have growing in pots.

Another fun job you can help with is picking fruit – just don't eat too much as you pick! Lots of berries and currants will ripen this month: gooseberries, redcurrants, blackcurrants and raspberries. Plums, nectarines, peaches and apricots are also in season.

When you've finished all your gardening jobs, find a lovely cool spot in the shade to rest. If you have two trees which are close enough together, you could ask an adult to help you put up a hammock, or you could make a canopy instead by tying some string between two trees and hanging a sheet over it. Put a rug or some cushions under the sheet and you have a beautiful, cool canopy where you can read a book or have an afternoon snooze – or eat some freshly picked fruit!

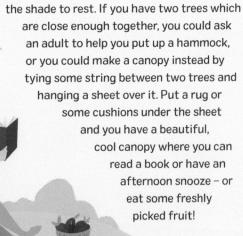

Recipe for *Perfect Plum Tart*

You will need:

Baking tray	500 g ready-made puff pastry
Greaseproof paper	140 g softened butter
Rolling pin	100 g caster sugar
Blunt knife	140 g ground almonds
Wooden spoon	25 g flaked almonds
Sharp knife	Plain flour for dusting
Food mixer	20 fresh, ripe plums
Wire rack	1 large egg
	Grated zest of 1 lemon
	½ teaspoon of almond extract

1. Heat the oven to 200°C/180°C fan/Gas Mark 6.
2. Line the baking tray with greaseproof paper.
3. Use the rolling pin to roll out the pastry until it is 3 mm thick and rectangle-shaped (40 cm x 30 cm). Carefully put it on the baking tray.
4. Use the blunt knife to make a line for the crust all the way around, about 1 cm in from the edge.
5. Bake the pastry for 12–15 minutes until it is lightly puffed and golden.
6. Remove the pastry from the oven and push the centre flat with the wooden spoon.
7. Ask an adult to help you halve the plums and remove the stones using the sharp knife.
8. Put the butter, sugar, ground almonds, egg, lemon zest and almond extract in the food mixer and beat them together until they make a paste. This is called 'frangipane'.
9. Spread the frangipane evenly over the pastry. Make sure you leave the crust clear.
10. Put the plum slices on top and sprinkle on some sugar and the flaked almonds.
11. Turn the oven down to 180°C/160°C fan/Gas Mark 4 and cook your plum tart for 30–40 minutes.
12. Let the tart cool on the wire rack, then slice and serve.

BUSY, BUZZY BEES!

There are more types of bee than you probably realised! Here are some of the ones you'll see in Britain.

Honeybee

Garden bumblebee

Patchwork leafcutter bee

Red mason bee

Red-tailed bumblebee

Common carder bee

Tree bumblebee

Honeybees are extremely important pollinators for flowers, fruits and vegetables. This means that they help other plants grow! Bees transfer pollen between the male and female parts of a plant, and plants can then grow seeds and fruit.

Top Five Bee Facts

★ There are more than 25,000 different species of bee in the world!
★ Male honeybees in the hive are called drones and they do not have a stinger.
★ Worker honeybees are females. They do all the different tasks needed to operate and maintain the hive.
★ An average beehive can hold around 50,000 honeybees.
★ The queen bee lays all of the eggs in a colony. At the height of the season, she may lay over 2,500 eggs per day!

DOWN ON THE RIVER

Swan Upping

During the third week of July, the
tradition of 'Swan Upping' takes place
on the River Thames. This is a ceremony in which mute swans are
caught by people in special boats called 'skiffs'. The swans are then
'ringed', which means they have numbered rings put on their legs so
that we know how many swans there are. They are then released
back to the river.

River Clean-Up

There are 'clean-ups' in rivers all over the UK. These are organised
events in which people come together to help clear away plastic and
other rubbish which sadly finds its way into rivers and streams and
causes all kinds of problems for the wildlife that lives there.

Getting involved in a clean-up is a lot of fun if you get together with
your friends and make a day of it. The events often happen in secret
natural spaces which you might not have been to before. It also
gives you a chance to help save the
environment and make life better
for wild animals. You can take the
plastic you find to recycling centres
or supermarkets which will take
plastic bags and film wrap as
well as bottles and cans.

If you want to find a clean-up near
you, go to **www.ukrivers.net** and
follow the links, or if you are near
the Thames or any of the rivers and
streams which flow into the Thames,
look at **www.thames21.org.uk** for
more information.

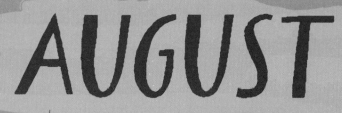

AUGUST

SPECIAL DAYS

1st Lammas/Lughnasadh (pagan celebrations)

2nd Summer bank holiday (Scotland)

10th Muharram (Islamic New Year)

22nd Raksha Bandhan (Hindu celebration)

29th Notting Hill Carnival

30th Summer bank holiday (England, Northern Ireland and Wales)

ANNIVERSARIES

85 years ago . . .

On 9 August 1936, Jesse Owens became the first American sprinter to win four gold medals at the Berlin Olympics.

95 years ago . . .

On 6 August 1926, Gertrude Ederle was the first woman to swim the English Channel. She completed the swim in 14 hours 31 minutes, beating the men's world record by 1 hour 59 minutes.

"In August when the days are hot, I like to find a shady spot."

In August, it can feel as though the summer holidays will stretch on forever. You can enjoy the long, sunny days and spend as much time outside as possible. Perhaps you will be lucky enough to go to another country for your holiday, but if not there is more than enough to do closer to home. Days by the seaside or down by the river or playing in the parks or woods near your home offer lots of opportunities for activities and fun things to do with your friends and family.

Or perhaps you are the sort of person who likes to do nothing at all on a hot, sunny day? Sometimes it's lovely just to find a spot of shade where you can read or snooze or sit and watch the world go by. Whatever you choose to do this August, make the most of all your free time and enjoy yourself!

Why is August Called August?

The Roman Emperor Augustus Caesar thought that since there was a month named after his great-uncle Julius there should be one named after him, too! So *Sextilis* or the 'sixth month' was changed to August in the year 8 BCE in his honour.

The Anglo-Saxons called it *Weodmonath*, which means 'weed month' as so many weeds grow at this time of year.

Birth Flower and Birthstone

The flower for this month is the poppy, which represents strength, love, marriage and family. The stone is called peridot. It is an unusual olive-green colour and contains a lot of iron. Peridot is formed in the magma of volcanoes and comes to the surface when volcanoes erupt.

Constellation of the Month

You can see the constellation of Pegasus in the east in the early evening. It is a square of four very bright stars with trailing 'legs' and a 'head' coming off it. The brightest of the four main stars is called *Epsilon Pegasi* and is an orange supergiant. The star's name in Arabic is *Enif*, meaning 'nose', because it marks the place where Pegasus's nose is meant to be.

DID YOU KNOW...

The name for the full moon this month is the Sturgeon Moon. Sturgeon are an endangered species of fish. If anyone catches one, they must return it to the water. Sturgeon can be huge, growing to double the size of a tall adult person. Males can live up to 55 years, and females can reach 150!

FESTIVAL FUN

1st August *Lammas*

Lammas is a pagan celebration of the first harvest, and is a time for giving thanks. The word *lammas* comes from the phrase 'loaf mass' which is a special celebration of the first grain to be cut in the harvest, and the first loaf to be made from that grain.

Lammas is also the name of the grain goddess, harvest queen and Earth mother. The harvest god is called John Barleycorn.

1st August *Lughnasadh*

On this day there is also an old Celtic festival called *Lughnasadh* – the festival of *Lugh* or *Lug*, the Celtic sun king and god of light. The celebrations include feasting, market fairs, games, bonfire celebrations and circle dancing. This is a time to remember that the power and energy of Lugh (the sun) is now slowing down and the darker days of winter are just around the corner.

10th August *Muharram*

Muharram is the Islamic New Year. The Islamic calendar is based on phases of the moon, and is 354 days long. This means that the date of the start of Muharram changes every year. During the month of Muharram, many Muslims fast and pray.

22nd August *Raksha Bandhan*

This is a Hindu festival celebrated at the full moon. The name *Raksha Bandhan* means the 'bond of protection'. *Raksha* means 'protection' and *Bandhan* means 'to tie'. The festival celebrates the relationship between brothers and sisters. During the festival, sisters tie a *rakhi* (holy thread) around their brothers' wrists as a symbol to show that they are praying for their brothers' protection and care. The brothers in return vow to look after their sisters, and give them a present.

The best time to tie rakhi on Raksha Bandhan is during *Aparahna*, which is late afternoon.

SPRING AND NEAP TIDES

A 'spring tide' does not only occur in the springtime! It is the name for the highest tide of the month, which in turn produces the lowest tide as its opposite. A 'neap tide' is the lowest high tide of the month and the highest low tide – this means that a neap tide shows the least difference between its high and low tides.

TOP TIP

It is a good idea to check the tides before you go swimming or take a boat out on the sea. You can do this online or you can buy tide times booklets from your local seaside town.

The moon affects the sea's tides. The tide changes every six hours, so if the tide is at its lowest (or the sea has 'gone out') at six in the morning, the tide will be at its highest again at midday.

ROCK POOLING

Who doesn't love the seaside on a hot summer's day? Even if you can't swim, perhaps you could find some rock pools to explore? The best time to do this is at low tide on a calm day when the sea has gone out and left water behind in the dips and hollows between the rocks. There's a lot to see in these miniature underwater worlds, so make sure you take your nature notebook with you – and try not to drop it in the water! Take a net and a bucket, too – that way you can take a closer look at some of the sea's minibeasts.

Remember to always be kind to the creatures you find and return them to their rock-pool homes after you have looked at them.

CAN YOU SPOT...

Porcelain crab

Sponge

Pipefish

Blenny

Shrimp

Butterfish

Green shore crab

Goby

Anemone

111

WATCH OUT, THERE'S A JELLY ABOUT!

No one likes to come across a jellyfish while they are swimming, so it is probably not going to be good news to you that we are seeing more and more of them on our beaches! This is because of climate change which is making our oceans warmer than they used to be, so jellyfish are able to move into areas that were once too cold for them. Also, the oxygen levels in the sea have fallen by about 2 per cent over the last 50 years, and this means that jellyfish now have the perfect environment in which to live. On top of all this, we have been taking too many fish out of the seas, so that fish such as tuna, which would normally eat jellyfish, are not such a danger to them any longer.

The six types of jellyfish found in British waters are:

Moon jellyfish
(UK-wide)

Compass jellyfish
(mainly in the South)

Blue jellyfish
(common in the South
West and Wales)

Lion's mane jellyfish
(North Wales, North
of Scotland)

Barrel jellyfish
(the South West, Ireland,
Wales, West of Scotland)

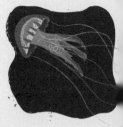

Mauve stinger jellyfish
(rare but can be found
along the south coast

DID YOU KNOW...

In Britain you are likely to see up to six different types of jellyfish and two species of jellyfish-like animals called the Portuguese man-of-war and the by-the-wind sailor. These last two are often confused with jellyfish but are actually 'siphonophores'.

UK jellyfish and siphonophores are not considered to be dangerous. However, some species can have a nasty sting. Their stings can range from mild, like the moon jellyfish, to very powerful, like the Portuguese man-of-war, which has the worst sting of all the jellyfish-like animals.

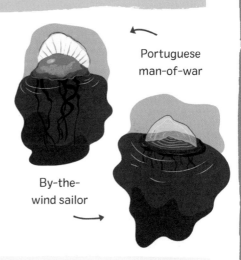

Portuguese man-of-war

By-the-wind sailor

If you are stung by a jellyfish, here are some things you can do to relieve the pain:

★ Use seawater to rinse the area that was stung. Don't use fresh water, as this will make the sting worse.

★ If you can see the stinging spines from the jellyfish on your skin, ask an adult to pull them off carefully with tweezers.

★ Applying heat helps: you could soak the area in very warm water (as hot as you can stand) or you could press a hot flannel or towel gently over the sting.

★ Painkillers such as paracetamol or ibuprofen will help, but never take these without asking an adult first.

★ If the pain isn't going away and it is very bad, you should go to a minor injuries unit.

CAMPING

Sleeping outdoors is one of the most fun activities for friends and family to enjoy during the warm summer months. You don't have to go away and stay on a campsite. If you have a garden, why not camp there? You can have just as much fun. And if you get a bit chilly, you can creep indoors and get back into your own bed! But after you've tried all these things, you won't want to go back inside . . .

1 Go on a nature walk

Once you have pitched your tent, go for a walk as the sun is setting. Listen to all the sounds around you. Which birds can you hear? What can you see? Try to walk around as quietly as you can so that you don't frighten any of the wildlife. You might hear owls or see a badger or a fox.

2 Cook over the campfire

This is the best bit about camping! Don't forget to pack a box of matches with your camping things. Then, while you are on your nature walk, gather some small, dry sticks. You can use these to start your fire. Stick a sausage on a skewer or make campfire bread by mixing flour, water and a pinch of salt into a thick dough and wrapping it around a clean stick. Then carefully hold the food over the flames until it is cooked. Marshmallows make a perfect dessert.

③ Tell stories and sing songs by the fire

Once you have had enough to eat, enjoy the warmth of the fire and the way the flames flicker and make shadows. It's just the right atmosphere for having a good singalong. Or maybe, if you're feeling brave, you could get someone to tell ghost stories! Always make sure that you put out the fire completely when you are finished by pouring water over the embers. Never light a fire during periods of very dry weather as it could get out of control.

④ Play torchlight tag

If you're getting a bit chilly, a game of tag will warm you up. Make sure you all have torches so that you don't trip over anything. It's fun to chase each other's torchlight in the dark!

⑤ Look at the stars

Before you crawl into your snug sleeping bag, look up at the night sky. You will know quite a lot about the constellations by now, so see if you can spot any of the ones you have learnt about in this book.

DRAGONFLIES

Dragonflies live for more than a year – some for up to five years, like the rare golden-ringed dragonfly – but very little of that time is spent as an adult dragonfly. There are three stages in the dragonfly life cycle: the egg, the nymph and the adult dragonfly. Most of its life cycle is spent under water as a nymph. If you are lucky, when you are pond dipping, you might find an old nymph case which has been left behind as the nymph grows and sheds its skin. It does this between 5 and 14 times until it is ready to change into a fully fledged dragonfly.

CAN YOU SPOT...

Scarce chaser*

Broad-bodied chaser

Norfolk hawker*

Common darter

Emperor

* Rare – only found in very specific areas and habitats.
All others can be found near ponds and lakes across the UK.
Visit **british-dragonflies.org.uk** to find out more!

Recipe for *Carrot Cake Muffins*

If you planted carrots in April, they will be ready to harvest now – just in time for you to make these delicious muffins!

You will need:

12 muffin cases
12-hole muffin tin
Food mixer
2 mixing bowls
Whisk
2 wooden spoons
Skewer
Wire rack
Sieve
Palette knife

175 g light muscovado sugar
100 g wholemeal self-raising flour
100 g white self-raising flour
1 teaspoon of bicarbonate of soda
2 teaspoons of mixed spice
Grated zest of 1 orange
2 eggs
150 ml sunflower oil
200 g carrots, grated
100 g butter, softened
300 g cream cheese
100 g icing sugar, sifted
1 teaspoon of vanilla extract
Orange sprinkles or carrot-cake decorations to serve

1 Heat oven to 180°C/160°C fan/ Gas Mark 4 and line the muffin tin with cases.

2 Mix together the sugar, flours, bicarbonate of soda, mixed spice and orange zest, using the food mixer.

3 Put the eggs and oil into one of the mixing bowls and whisk them together.

4 Pour the eggs and oil into the dry ingredients, add the grated carrot and combine them with a wooden spoon. Do not overmix – the muffins will be lighter if you don't mix everything in too much.

5 Divide the mixture between the muffin cases.

6 Bake for 20–22 minutes until a skewer poked in comes out clean.

7 Cool on the wire rack while you make the icing.

8 In the second mixing bowl, beat the butter with a wooden spoon until it's really soft.

9 Beat the cream cheese, sieved icing sugar and vanilla extract into the butter.

10 Swirl the icing on top of the muffins, using the palette knife to smooth it, then sprinkle with decorations.

SEPTEMBER

SPECIAL DAYS

1st Start of autumn

6th Rosh Hashanah (Jewish festival)

10th Ganesh Chaturthi (Hindu festival)

16th Yom Kippur (Jewish holiday)

22nd Autumn equinox/Mabon (pagan celebration)/Harvest festival (Christian celebration)

29th Michaelmas Day (Christian celebration)

ANNIVERSARIES

20 years ago . . .

On 11 September 2001, the World Trade Centre in New York came crashing down after two planes flew into it. The day is remembered as '9/11' and there is a memorial where the towers once stood.

75 years ago . . .

On 5 September 1946, Freddie Mercury, the lead singer of the rock band Queen, was born.

355 years ago . . .

On 2 September 1666, the Great Fire of London broke out in a small bakery on a street called Pudding Lane in London. The fire raged for four days and destroyed most of the city.

*"Every leaf speaks bliss to me
Fluttering from the autumn tree."*

EMILY BRONTË (1818–1848)

September can be a golden month. Summer is fading, yes, but there is still warmth in the air, and the leaves on the trees are slowly turning from their different shades of green to the fiery colours of autumn. And, of course, the end of summer means the beginning of school again, which not everyone is happy about! But the days are still long enough to allow some time for fun in the park after school, so make the most of it before the clocks change and the countdown to winter begins.

Why is September Called September?

This month kept its original name from the Roman calendar.
September comes from the Latin word *septem,*
which means 'seven'. September was the seventh
month in the year when the calendar began
with March instead of January.

Constellation of the Month

Cygnus means 'swan' in Latin. The Romans took the
word from the Greek *kyknos*. The ancient Greeks
had many stories about swans. One of them
was about the tragic hero Orpheus. He was
killed and then transformed into a swan,
after which he was placed in the sky.
The constellation of Cygnus is
quite easy to spot as it is shaped
like a cross. It is in fact sometimes
known as the Northern Cross.

September Birth Signs

People born from 23rd August to 22nd September
are said to be born under the sign of Virgo. They're
supposed to be loyal, kind, hard-working and
practical. They can also be worriers, are often
shy and can end up working too hard if they don't
make time to relax. They like animals, reading and
nature and they don't like rude people! (Who does?)

People with birthdays on or between 23rd
September to 22nd October are born under the
sign of Libra. The sign is depicted by a set of
weighing scales which represent a balanced
personality. Librans are lovers of peace and
harmony. Unfortunately, this means that they
sometimes can't make up their minds as they
can usually see both sides to every argument!

FESTIVAL FUN

If you found it hard to stick to your New Year's resolutions, you could try starting again in September! This month is a time for new beginnings for some religions. It is also time to give thanks for nature's gift to us of the harvest.

6th September *Rosh Hashanah*

This is a very important Jewish festival as it celebrates the start of the New Year in the Hebrew calendar. It is also a time for giving thanks for the birth of the universe and the day on which God created Adam and Eve. People light candles, enjoy special meals and come together to pray.

10th September *Ganesh Chaturthi*

Today is the day that Hindus start celebrating the birthday of Lord Ganesha, the god with the head of an elephant. Communities get together to worship, have parties and decorate their houses with models and pictures of Lord Ganesha. He is known as the god of new beginnings and is supposed to bring prosperity, good fortune and success.

DID YOU KNOW...

According to some stories in Hindu mythology, the moon laughed at Ganesha for having such a large stomach. Ganesha got angry and declared that from that day, if anyone looked at the moon on Ganesh Chaturthi, they would fall over.

16th September *Yom Kippur*

This is the holiest day of the year for Jewish people. It is a day for saying sorry for things you have done wrong and asking for forgiveness. Jews traditionally wear white and they fast and pray for up to 25 hours. They often spend most of the day in the synagogue.

22nd September *Mabon or Harvest Festival*

The harvest festival is the closest thing we have to a day of thanksgiving in Britain. The word 'harvest' comes from the Old English word *hærfest* meaning 'autumn'. This was a very important time of year, as the success of the harvest could mean the difference between life or death for a whole community. In the past, even children had to help bring in the harvest. Then, as soon as it was over, everyone would return from the fields for the harvest supper. This was a huge feast with much singing and laughter.

29th September *Michaelmas Day*

The Christian celebration of Michaelmas, or the 'Feast of St Michael and All Angels' falls near the equinox. Traditionally, Michaelmas Day was the time when new servants were hired or land was bought or sold, and money was paid back to people who had lent it. This is why most schools and universities start their new year around September; some of them even call the autumn term 'Michaelmas Term'.

YOU SAY TOMATO...

Is the tomato a fruit or a vegetable? People have been arguing about this for hundreds of years: in America in 1887 the argument went all the way to the US Supreme Court! This sounds silly, but it was quite important because if it was decided that tomatoes were vegetables, they would be more expensive.

In actual fact, the tomato is a fruit because it contains seeds and grows on a vine. The same is true of cucumbers, squashes, beans and peas. But, of course, everyone thinks of them as vegetables because they are served in savoury dishes and not as desserts!

We can get tomatoes all year round, but when growing your own, the best time to pick them is often in late August or early September. While the days are still golden and warm, it's lovely to throw your own tomatoes into a salad. As the month wears on, you might be left with a few that are not so nice to eat raw, but they are great for soups, sauces and chutneys, and can be cooked in stews and tarts.

Recipe for *Tasty Tomato Tarts*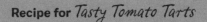

These small tarts are great in packed lunches or for taking on picnics.

You will need:

Food processor
4 small tart cases
Greaseproof paper
Baking beans
Mixing bowl
Whisk
Wire rack

175 g plain flour
85 g butter
85 g strong cheddar cheese, grated
3 eggs
4 tablespoons of Dijon mustard
4 tablespoons of crème fraiche
250 g cherry tomatoes, cut in half
Sprig of fresh thyme

1. Heat the oven to 180°C/fan 160°C/Gas Mark 4.
2. Whizz up the flour, butter and cheese in the food processor until the mixture looks like breadcrumbs.
3. Add one egg and whizz again until the pastry forms a ball.
4. Use the pastry to line the four tart cases, then pop them in the fridge and let them chill for 10 minutes.
5. Take the pastry cases out of the fridge and line them with squares of greaseproof paper.
6. Fill the cases with some of the baking beans and bake them for 7–10 minutes until the pastry looks dry.
7. Remove the paper and baking beans and continue to cook the pastry cases for 2–3 minutes more, until they look golden, then take them out of the oven.
8. Whisk the remaining eggs into the Dijon mustard and crème fraiche.
9. Scatter the halved cherry tomatoes into the tart cases and sprinkle the thyme leaves over the top.
10. Pour the egg mixture almost up to the top of each tart case, but leave a little space as it will rise slightly while cooking.
11. Bake for 10 minutes, then turn the oven down to 150°C/fan 130°C/Gas Mark 3 and bake for a further 15 minutes until the egg mixture is just set.
12. Cool on the wire rack before serving.

BONKERS FOR CONKERS

'Conkers' is the name of a traditional game that is played using the seeds from the horse chestnut tree.

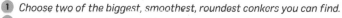

Prepare Your Conkers

1. *Choose two of the biggest, smoothest, roundest conkers you can find.*
2. *Ask an adult to make a hole through the centre of each one, either with a nail or a screwdriver, or even a drill.*
3. *Take two long pieces of string or garden twine – about 20 cm long – and thread a piece through the hole in each conker. Make sure you tie a knot in the bottom so that the conkers don't just slide off!*
4. *Find a friend and challenge them to a game . . .*

TOP TIP

When playing, hold the conker low, away from your face, and never flick or throw a conker near someone else's face.

How to Play

★ Stand opposite each other, holding the end of the string so that the conkers are hanging down

★ Take it in turns to hit your conker against your opponent's.

★ The conker that breaks the other one gains a point.

WILD SEA, WILD ME

Believe it or not, September is the best month to go for a swim in the sea. This is because the water has been warming up over the summer and it is now as warm as it will be all year. If you do fancy a dip, take a grown-up with you and be careful to check the tides beforehand. Make sure you are swimming in a safe area where you can get in and out easily. Also take a good look at the waves first, as the sea can begin to get quite stormy and rough in September.

BE A NATURE DETECTIVE

Walk carefully through the woods, keeping your eyes open for any signs of where an animal has been. You might notice some leaves have been disturbed, or there is a hole under a fence where a creature has pushed its way through.

Look for a good print that shows you a lot of detail. You might need to gently push any leaves or sticks aside.

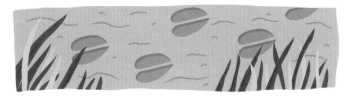

You could take photos of any footprints that you find, but why not make drawings of them, too? Drawing makes us concentrate harder on what we are seeing because we have to look closely to copy the details of the print. Just like a wildlife expert, you will learn and remember what the tracks look like if you ever see them again.

You can then take your drawings home and compare them with the animal print guide on the opposite page. Can you identify the animals from their prints? Be sure to also make a note of the plants and the kind of landscape where you found the tracks. You can use your nature notebook for this. This will help you remember where you found the marks and to identify the animal, too.

Animal Print Guide

Badger

Deer

Squirrel

Duck

Fox

Hedgehog

Otter

Rabbit

Dog

Shrew

Swan

Crow

Mouse

Pigeon

Make a *Lord Ganesh Model*

During the festival of Ganesh Chaturthi, many Hindus decorate their homes with images and models of Lord Ganesh, the elephant god. It is quite easy to make a model using salt dough, and you can paint it when it's dry. There are lots of recipes online for how to make salt dough. You might need to use wooden toothpicks to hold the sections of the model together.

Here are the steps to follow to make the model:

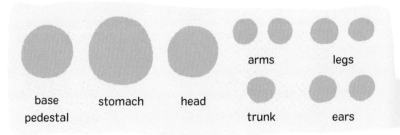

base
pedestal   stomach   head   arms   legs

trunk   ears

1 Make your dough and divide it into balls for the various body parts, as shown above.

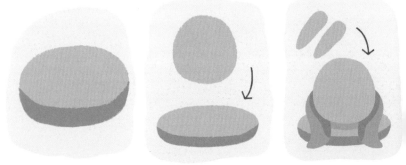

2 Flatten the base pedestal piece of salt dough into a circle. This is what Lord Ganesh will sit on.

3 Roll the stomach piece of dough into a ball. Place it on the circle.

4 Roll out two little sausage-shaped pieces to make the legs and bend them around the body, as shown in the picture.

5 Roll out the arms in the same way as the legs and bend them around the body, as shown in the picture.

6 Insert a toothpick into the body and fix the head to it.

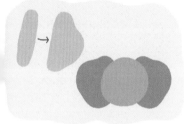

7 Roll out the sausage shapes for ears and then pull them into the shape of elephant ears. Fix them to either side of the head.

8 Roll out the trunk and bend it and fix it to the front of the face. Use a toothpick to make eyes and to draw on tusks.

9 Now you need to give Lord Ganesh a crown! You can do this with more dough or make him a crown out of coloured paper.

TOP TIP
If you want to paint your model, the best paint to use is acrylic.

OCTOBER

SPECIAL DAYS

19th   Prophet's birthday (Muslim celebration)

21st   Apple Day

31st   Samhain Eve (pagan festival)/All Saints' Eve (Christian festival)/Halloween/ Daylight saving ends

ANNIVERSARIES

50 years ago . . .

On 10 October 1971, London Bridge was reopened in Lake Havasu City, Arizona, after it had been sold, taken down from its place in London and shipped over the Atlantic to the USA!

955 years ago . . .

On 14 October 1066, the Battle of Hastings was fought. William the Conqueror and his army defeated the English and killed King Harold II, the last Anglo-Saxon king of England.

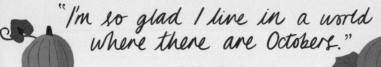

"I'm so glad I live in a world where there are Octobers."

L. M. MONTGOMERY (1874–1942)

October leads us gently into autumn. The days are still mild and the light is golden as it reflects off the turning leaves. The colours are glorious! This is the perfect time of year to go out walking in the countryside and parks. Run through the fallen leaves and look out for especially beautiful colours and shapes. Maybe you could collect your favourite leaves and press them? Pressed autumn leaves make brilliant decorations on cards or bookmarks.

DID YOU KNOW...

In Munich, in the south of Germany, there is a festival every year called Oktoberfest. The first one was held from 12–17 October 1810 to celebrate the marriage of King Ludwig I to Princess Therese von Sachsen-Hildburghausen. Nowadays, the festival starts in September.

Why is October Called October?

October gets its name from the Latin word *octo* which means 'eight', and was named by the Romans during a time when the calendar year began with March instead of with January as it does now.

The Anglo-Saxon name for this month was *Winterfylleth* which comes from the words for winter and the full moon.

Phases of the Moon in October 2021

New Moon	First Quarter	Full Moon	Last Quarter
6th October	13th October	20th October	28th October

The Moon's a Balloon!

The October full moon this year is called the Hunter's Moon. It is also known as the Blood Moon because it can often be a striking red or orange colour. Of course, the colour of the actual moon hasn't changed! The moon hangs lower in the sky at this time of year, closer to the horizon, and so we are seeing it through more of the Earth's atmosphere. The gases around the Earth and the tiny particles in the air affect the way in which we see light. Orange and red light has longer wavelengths and so these are the colours we see reflected off the moon when it is closer to us.

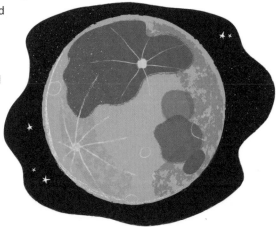

FESTIVAL FUN

19th October *Prophet's Birthday*

In the UK and all over the world, some Muslims see this as a day to celebrate. In some countries there are street parades, the mosques are decorated and children read out poems about the Prophet's life. People can spend the day donating food and money to charity, too. Other Muslims see this day as a time for concentrating on the holy book, the *Qur'an*.

31st October *Samhain Eve*

The festival of Samhain (pronounced 'Saah-win' or 'saah-ween') comes from ancient pagan Celtic and Gaelic harvest traditions. Its name means 'summer's end'. It is a time for giving thanks for the end of the harvest and it marks the beginning of the coldest half of the year.

Pagans celebrate by holding a feast and by remembering those loved ones who have died and are no longer with us. Sometimes people set a place at the table for these loved ones and put food in front of it as an offering to those who have passed on.

31st October *All Saints' Eve*

This is a Christian festival also known as All Hallows' Eve, Hallowed Evening or Holy Evening, which is how we get the name Halloween! On the evening of 31st October, some Christians begin three days of ceremonies and services to remember loved ones who have died and the saints ('hallowed' or holy people). It is traditional to light candles for those who have died and to spend time praying and remembering them.

31st October *Halloween*

Nowadays, we associate Halloween with fun and games and dressing-up. But in fact, as far back as the 16th century, people had parties on 31st October, playing games and practising rituals to try and tell the future, especially about deaths or marriages in the family. This is where the game of apple-bobbing comes from. It used to be thought that the first person to bite into an apple would be the first person to get married!

Before pumpkins were brought over from America, people would use turnips or other root vegetables to make lanterns. These were carved with ugly faces in the hope that they would scare away evil spirits.

PUMPKIN CARVING

How about carving your own lantern? These look great as table decorations for a Halloween party or you can leave them outside your house to welcome trick-or-treaters.

You will need:

Medium-sized pumpkin
Chopping board
Sharp knife
Large metal spoon
Medium bowl

Biro or marker pen
Tealight
Wooden toothpicks (optional)
Scary Halloween vampire teeth
(optional)

1. *Ask an adult to help you cut a small 'lid' off the top of your pumpkin.*
2. *Use the metal spoon to remove the seeds and scoop out as much of the flesh as you can.*
3. *Put the seeds and flesh in the bowl and put aside.*
4. *Draw a face on your pumpkin.*
5. *Ask an adult to help you cut out the eyes, nose and mouth. You could add wooden toothpicks and scary vampire teeth.*
6. *Ask an adult to help you light the tealight and put it in your pumpkin.*
7. *Turn out all the lights! Your super-scary pumpkin lantern is spookily ready for Halloween!*

TOP TIP

Use the flesh you have scooped out to make pumpkin muffins or pumpkin soup. You can also roast the seeds for a tasty snack!

MONSTER BOWLING!

This is a great game for all ages. You can have a lot of fun preparing for it too.

You will need:

Old food cans, washed with their labels removed
Coloured paints
Brushes

White loo paper
Tennis ball
Small prize (a sweet, for example)

1. *Once the cans are clean and dry, give them a good coat of paint. Purple, orange and green are great Halloween colours. Use white if you want the can to look like a zombie or a mummy!*
2. *Use black paint to add the eyes, noses and mouths.*
3. *Wrap white loo paper around a can to make it mummified!*
4. *To play the game, stack the decorated cans in a pyramid.*
5. *Get your friends to line up to take turns to throw the ball. You'll need to decide how far back you want them to stand – the further away, the harder it will be to knock down the cans.*
6. *Restack the cans in between turns and keep a tally of how many cans each person has knocked down.*
7. *You could award a small prize to the person who knocks down the most cans.*

BLACK HISTORY MONTH

Black History Month is in October in Britain. It's when people celebrate the contributions that black people have made to the country. The idea for Black History Month originally came from the USA and it is still celebrated there in February every year.

The American historian Carter G. Woodson came up with the idea. He had found that Americans knew a lot about the history of white people in their country, but that no one seemed to speak or write about the history of black Americans. He wanted people to be properly educated so that black people would no longer be discriminated against and treated badly because of the colour of their skin, so he set up the Association for the Study of Negro Life and History in 1915 which encouraged historians to research and write about black history and culture.

Ignatius Sancho

Mary Prince

In the 1970s, a man called Akyaaba Addai-Sebo went from Britain to America and was inspired by Black History Month. He thought that Britain should be celebrating it, too, so he started the British version in 1987.

Black History Month is a time for celebration and remembrance, and there are many wonderful talks, food festivals and musical events you can go to – everything that celebrates the achievements, culture and contributions from black people to our lives today.

DID YOU KNOW...

It is believed that Black History Month is celebrated in October in Britain because traditionally, October is when African chiefs and leaders gather to settle their differences, so Akyaaba chose this month to reconnect with African roots.

Mary Seacole

Rosa Parks

Martin Luther King Jr.

APPLES GALORE

October is apple month! If you live in an area where there are a lot of apple trees, you might find lots of apples falling into the street. These are known as 'windfalls'. They might look battered and bruised, but windfalls are excellent apples to put in pies, crumbles and cakes. They make delicious apple sauce as well, which is yummy as a dessert with ice cream or yoghurt and also goes very well with roast pork. Always check windfalls carefully as there are a lot of sleepy wasps around at this time of year and they can sometimes be found slowly munching their way through apples that have fallen to the ground. You will also need to wash windfalls and cut out any bruised flesh before you use them for cooking.

Apple Day takes place on 21st October to celebrate apples and orchards!

142

Recipe for *Easy Apple Chutney*

You will need:

Large heavy saucepan
Wooden spoon
Glass jars (about 10, depending on the size of each jar)
Greaseproof paper
Colourful fabric or wrapping paper and rubber bands
Sticky labels

1½ kg cooking apples, peeled and diced
750 g light muscovado sugar
500 g raisins
2 medium onions, finely chopped
2 teaspoons of mustard seeds
2 teaspoons of ground ginger
1 teaspoon of salt
700 ml cider or malt vinegar

1. Put all the ingredients in the large saucepan.
2. Give everything a good stir with the wooden spoon.
3. Bring the mixture to a boil over a medium heat.
4. Leave it to simmer for about 30–40 minutes with the lid off and stir occasionally.
5. Once the mixture is thick and pulpy, remove the pan from the heat.
6. Leave the chutney to cool before transferring it into sterilised, clean, dry jars.
7. Put circles of greaseproof paper on the top of the chutney before screwing on the lids.
8. Cut out circles of fabric or wrapping paper about 2 cm larger than the lids.
9. Cover the lids with the fabric or paper and hold them in place with rubber bands.
10. Write on the sticky labels so that you know what is in the jars – you could add your name so that everyone knows who made it, e.g. Anna's Apple Chutney.

TOP TIP
Leave the window open when you are cooking the chutney as the vinegary smell can fill the room!

TIME FOR BED

As well as birds and animals migrating, autumn is a time for some of them to hibernate, which means they go to sleep for the whole winter. There are not many creatures that do this in Britain, as our winters are not as cold as in other parts of the world.

Why Do Animals Hibernate?

It's not just because they like being warm and cosy – or lazy! Animals who hibernate aren't simply going to sleep – their bodies have adapted to make sure that they survive during the winter months. When they go into hibernation, their bodies slow right down so that they breathe more slowly, their hearts beat much more slowly and the temperature of their bodies drops. This means that they don't need to eat so much because their bodies are not using as much energy as when they are awake and running around. However, before they hibernate they make sure they eat lots and lots to fatten up so that they have plenty of energy in reserve during their long sleep.

TOP TIP

You can help hedgehogs in your garden by leaving out tinned dog or cat food (just avoid fish!)

THE DARK IS RISING

The days are getting shorter and shorter. However, we still have light evenings until the clocks change on 31st October. This means we get an extra hour in bed the night before. It can be confusing if you are a baby or a pet as it messes around with your mealtimes!

Why Do the Clocks Change?

We didn't always bother with changing the clocks. In the old days, people went to bed when the sun went down and got up again when it rose. Midday was several minutes earlier in the east of the country than it was in the south, and several minutes later in the west. This meant that town clocks across the British Isles showed different times. The building of the railway network changed all that because the time had to be the same all over the country, or people would not have had the faintest idea when to catch a train.

Then a man called William Willett suggested to parliament that if the clocks changed, we would all enjoy more daylight in the autumn and winter months. So, since 1916, the clocks have gone back one hour in October and in March the clocks have been put forward by one hour. This is known as 'daylight saving'.

TOP TIP

In spring, the clocks spring forward an hour, and in the autumn, they fall back.

NOVEMBER

SPECIAL DAYS

1st   All Saints' Day (Christian celebration)

2nd   All Souls' Day (Christian celebration)

4th   Diwali (Hindu New Year)

5th   Guy Fawkes Night (Bonfire Night)

11th   Armistice Day (Remembrance Day)/Martinmas

14th   Remembrance Sunday

21st   Stir-up Sunday (last Sunday before Advent)

28th   First Sunday of Advent (Christian celebration)/
First day of Hanukkah (Jewish celebration)

30th   St Andrew's Day (Scotland)

ANNIVERSARIES

25 years ago...

On 30 November 1996, the Stone of Scone was brought to Edinburgh Castle, 700 years after it was removed from Scotland by King Edward I of England.

365 years ago...

On 8 November 1656, the English astronomer and physicist Edmond Halley was born. Halley's Comet is named after him – a comet which was last seen in 1986 and will next be visible in 2061!

"November's sky is chill and drear."

We can no longer deny it – winter is on its way! The shortest day is less than two months away, so it is no wonder that so many festivals this month celebrate light. Many festivals also focus on sweet-tasting food – a sweet treat can be just what you need when you've been outside, battling the cold! This is the time of year to tidy away the garden for winter, and a bonfire is a great way to get rid of dead leaves and wood.

Why is November Called November?

The word 'November' comes from the Latin word for the number nine, *novem*. This is because, just like September and October before it, November keeps its name from a time when the calendar had only 10 months.

The Anglo-Saxons called this month *Blotmonath,* which means 'blood month'. This is because it was traditional at this time of year to kill farm animals and preserve the meat for the winter months ahead.

Constellation of the Month

Taurus is the Latin word for 'bull'. Look out for this constellation in the east, where it starts the night low in the sky. If you look for the bright orange giant star called Aldebaran, that will help you find the rest of the constellation.

November Birth Signs

People born under the sign of Scorpio
(the scorpion) on or between 23rd October and
21st November are said to be brave, passionate,
stubborn and a true friend. They like the truth,
facts and being right! They also like to have deep,
long-lasting friendships.

Sagittarius is represented by a centaur – a mythological
creature who is half-man, half-horse. People born
under the sign of Sagittarius, on or between 22nd
November and 21st December, are supposed to be
generous and have a great sense of humour.
They can also be very impatient and will
often speak first and think after!

DID YOU KNOW...

The full moon this month is sometimes known as the Beaver
Moon. The name comes from Northern Native American
culture and was chosen because beavers build their dams
at this time of the year to get ready for the cold season.
Another name for the November full moon is the Frost Moon.

FESTIVAL FUN

4th November *Diwali*

Diwali marks the start of the Hindu New Year. Sikhs and Jains also celebrate at this time. Diwali is five days long, and on the third day, many Hindus light special oil lamps called *diyas*. The lamps symbolise the triumph of light over darkness, good over evil, and knowledge over ignorance. Many gods – including Rama and his wife, Sita, and Lakshmi, the goddess of wealth and prosperity – are celebrated with music, *puja* (prayers), firework displays and by sharing traditional sweets.

5th November *Guy Fawkes or Bonfire Night*

"Remember, remember the 5th of November, Gunpowder, treason and plot!"

This is an annual commemoration of the day in 1605 when a man called Guy Fawkes was arrested for being a part of the 'Gunpowder Plot'. The plot was thought up by a group of men who wanted to blow up King James I and the Houses of Parliament in London. Guy Fawkes was found hiding beneath the House of Lords, guarding some explosives. Thankfully, the bombs never went off.

Nowadays, people spend the evening going to firework displays, standing around a big bonfire and eating hot dogs! It is a great way to chase away the winter blues.

11th November *Armistice Day (Remembrance Day)*

Armistice Day or Remembrance Day is a time for remembering all those who were killed in the First and Second World Wars and other wars that have since followed. A two-minute silence is held to remember the dead on the Sunday nearest to 11th November. People traditionally wear a red poppy around this time to show that they have not forgotten the people who died in the war.

21st November *Stir-up Sunday*

This is the last Sunday before Advent, which is the period of time in which Christians prepare for Christmas, and is the day people traditionally make their Christmas puddings. In the old days, it was a time for families to get together to mix and steam the pudding. Everyone would take a turn to stir the pudding and make a special wish for the year ahead.

28th November *First Sunday of Advent*

Advent lasts for four Sundays leading up to Christmas. Advent always begins on the Sunday that falls between 27th November and 3rd December. In churches, Christians light one candle every Sunday of Advent. It is common for people to also begin their own countdown to Christmas on 1st December with Advent calendars or Advent candles which have the numbers 1 to 24 on them.

28th November – 6th December *Hanukkah*

Sometimes spelled *Chanukah*, this Jewish festival lasts for eight days. During this time, Jewish people remember how the Second Temple in Jerusalem was dedicated to God. Hanukkah is often called the 'festival of lights' because the holiday is celebrated with the lighting of the *menorah* candlestick. Traditional foods are served, such as potato pancakes and jam-filled doughnuts called *sufganiyot*.

REMEMBER, REMEMBER... HEDGEHOGS

★ If you are having a bonfire for Bonfire Night, it is best to pile up the leaves and wood on the actual day of the bonfire. If you do it too far in advance, a hedgehog might think you have made a lovely place in which it can hibernate.

★ You can stop hedgehogs from finding their way into a bonfire pile by building a small fence with chicken wire around the edge. The wire should be about 1 metre high and should be held in place with bamboo sticks. Try to make the wire slope outwards – this will stop the hedgehogs from trying to climb in.

★ If you have already helped make a nice mound of garden waste to burn, perhaps you could move it to another place for the actual bonfire? This will give you a chance to look through the leaves and so on to make sure that there are no hedgehogs hiding inside the pile.

★ Just in case you have missed a hedgehog, make sure the adult in charge of the bonfire lights the pile on one side only and keeps away from the unlit side. That way, any hiding hedgehogs have a chance of escaping to safety.

TOP TIP

Never feed a hedgehog bread and milk! This can upset its tummy. In the wild, hedgehogs eat slugs and insects.

★ Finally, if you do find a hedgehog, put on some gardening gloves (or oven gloves) before touching its spiky little body. This is also to protect the hedgehog as they don't like getting the smell of humans on them!

★ Then, when you scoop up the creature, make sure you pick it up along with any leaves or bedding it has pulled around itself. Hedgehogs make cosy little nests, and you don't want to undo all their hard work.

★ Put the hedgehog, with its nest, in a high-sided cardboard box with plenty of newspaper or old towels. You'll need to put a lid on, too – remember to make some air holes in the lid so that the hedgehog can breathe.

★ Put the box in a quiet, safe place such as a shed or garage well away from noise. Once your bonfire is over, release the hedgehog into the wild again. Let it go under a hedge, bush or behind a stack of logs so that it feels safe.

DID YOU KNOW...

The number of hedgehogs in Britain is falling fast. To find out more about how to help hedgehogs, visit **www.britishhedgehogs.org.uk**

BRILLIANT BEETLES

There are more types of beetle than any other type of insect. In Britain there are about 4,000 species, and they make up 40 per cent of insect life in this country. It is thought that there are around 350,000 beetle species worldwide.

CAN YOU SPOT...

7-spot ladybird

This is one of the most familiar beetles and you have probably seen a lot of them. They are very useful to gardeners as they like to eat greenfly (also known as aphids).

Stag beetle

This is Britain's largest beetle, but you may never see one as it spends most of its life below ground feeding on dead wood. Male stag beetles have 'antlers' which are actually large jaws.

Green tiger beetle

This scary-looking minibeast has long legs and sharp jaws. It takes short flying leaps to attack its prey or to escape danger.

Violet ground beetle

This beetle is large and moves very fast. It goes out mainly at night and can be found in woods, meadows and gardens. If it is frightened, it gives off a nasty smell.

Cockchafer

This beetle is mostly nocturnal. Sometimes it is known as the May bug because it comes out in the spring.

Devil's coach-horse

This large beetle looks like a mini monster! It likes damp places so will mostly be found under logs and stones. It can give you a nasty nip, so be careful.

Oil beetle

These large insects get their name from their shiny, oily appearance. They are usually found in the spring on meadow flowers.

STARS OF THE EVENING

Have you ever been out for a walk, or on a long car journey, and seen a black mass of birds swooping and circling in the sky? If so, you have probably seen a 'murmuration' of starlings. It is the most amazing sight – like a swirling black cloud of birds that is constantly on the move. The birds perform incredible acrobatic stunts and the flock makes breathtaking patterns in the sky.

Murmurations become more common in November. More and more birds will flock together as the month goes on. Starlings choose places to roost together that are well sheltered from bad weather and predators. This means that they like woodlands, reed beds, cliffs and even disused buildings, too.

There are some beautiful places in Britain that have fantastic spots for watching murmurations: Gretna Green in Scotland and Brighton Pier are two of the more famous ones.

DID YOU KNOW...

The number of starlings roosting in one place can grow to as many as 750,000! They group together for safety, as predators such as hawks and peregrine falcons find it much harder to hunt down one bird in the middle of the huge hypnotising flocks. They also come together to keep warm at night and possibly to 'talk' to each other about where the best feeding areas are!

SEE THE SEALS

There are two types of seal found around the British coast: the common seal and the grey seal. The common seal gives birth to pups in the summer, whereas the grey seal has its babies in November. The grey seal spends a lot of time in the sea, where it hunts for fish, squid, crab and lobster. They live in large family groups called 'colonies' which can be made up of thousands of seals.

★ The grey seal prefers the rocky coasts found in northern and western parts of the country and is most likely to be seen off the coast of Northumberland, Lincolnshire, the Orkney Islands and Cornwall.

★ The grey seal grows to a much larger size than the common seal and males are much bigger than females.

★ The grey seal has a much longer nose or 'snout' than the common seal and has nostrils spaced further apart!

★ Seals like to leave the water to rest and bask in the sun after they have been hunting.

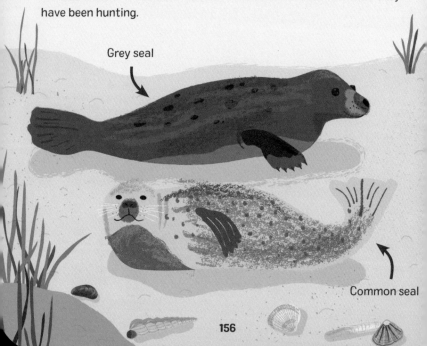

Grey seal

Common seal

PRETTY PEBBLES

Whenever you pick up a pebble on a beach, you are holding the story of Planet Earth in your hand! Pebbles begin as chunks of rock that break off from cliffs, or are brought down to the sea by rivers. Some of them come from man-made things such as glass. Pebbles are formed by the way they are bashed about as they fall or the way they are worn smooth by water. Some of them have shiny flecks that glint in the sun. Some are dark and dense. When they are wet, you may see strange and wonderful textures and patterns inside them.

DID YOU KNOW...

A pebble is a stone that is no larger than a tennis ball and no smaller than a pea. Anything bigger is a stone or rock and anything smaller is gravel, shingle or sand.

Conglomerate

Sea glass

Spotted slate

Quartz veinstone

Granite

Sandstone

Serpentine

Schist

Jasper

Flint

Quartz breccia

Pink feldspar veins

THE COLOURS OF NATURE

Sometimes during winter walks the weather is not great and you are trudging along in the mud, wishing you were tucked up snug indoors instead. A good idea to make walks more fun is to play games on your way. See if you can get the grown-ups to join in! You are bound to be faster than they are . . .

This is a fun activity to do on a winter walk. You might think that there are not many colours around at this time of the year – after all, there are fewer flowers around now and most of the autumn leaves have fallen from the trees. It might look quite bleak and bare outside – all brown and grey and boring.

Is it, though? Next time you go for a walk, try this activity. It might change your mind about how boring the natural world looks in winter! You can either complete the activity outside or, if it's a chilly day, bring your treasures home to finish.

You will need:

Paint chart (free of charge from most DIY stores)
Bag or large pockets!

1 Look out for any small items you can find: sticks, stones, nut shells, leaves, wild seed heads, feathers, bark and pine cones.

2 Put these items carefully in your bag or pockets.

3 Once you think you have enough items, find a sheltered place to stop.

4 Lay the colour chart out on the ground or on a picnic table.

5 Lay the items you have found next to the chart.

6 Look carefully at the chart – can you match your items to the colours on it?

7 How many different browns, greens, greys, yellows, reds and oranges have you found? Have you found any other colours?

DECEMBER

SPECIAL DAYS

6th   Last day of Hanukkah

21st   Winter solstice/Midwinter/Yule (pagan celebration)/Start of winter

24th   Christmas Eve/First day of Christmas (Christian celebration)

25th   Christmas Day (Christian celebration)

26th   Boxing Day

31st   New Year's Eve/Hogmanay (Scotland)

ANNIVERSARIES

30 years ago . . .

On 16 December 1991, Stella Rimington became the first woman to be made Director General of the security service known as MI5.

75 years ago . . .

On 18 December 1946, the American film director Steven Spielberg was born. He is best known for films such as *Jaws*, *E.T.* and *Jurassic Park*.

260 years ago . . .

On 1 December 1761, the French creator of wax sculptures Marie Tussaud was born. In 1835, she brought her wax sculptures to Baker Street in London, which is where the waxwork museum Madame Tussauds stands to this day.

> *"I heard a bird sing*
> *In the dark of December."*

OLIVER HERFORD (1863–1935)

In Britain, Christmas has become the main focus of this month. It is not the only festival going on, though. There are lots of other celebrations of light during this month because it contains the shortest day of the year. For many thousands of years, people have spent dark December thinking ahead to a time when the sun will come back. Whichever festival you celebrate, you are bound to have lots of fun, food and treats!

Why is December Called December?

This month gets its name from the Latin word for tenth, *decem*. The Anglo-Saxons called December *Ærra Geola* or the month 'before Yule'. Yule was an important winter festival and is still celebrated today by pagans. Many of the 'Yuletide' traditions have found their way into things we now think of as Christmas traditions.

Phases of the Moon **in December 2021**

New Moon	**First Quarter**	**Full Moon**	**Last Quarter**
4th December	11th December	19th December	27th December

The full moon this month is known as the Cold Moon or Long Night Moon.

WHATEVER THE WEATHER

December may be the start of winter, but by the end of the month the days are already getting longer. It is because of this promise of longer, lighter days that the longest night has traditionally been a time for celebration. The dark can be sad or scary sometimes, but just think: if there was no darkness, there would be no light! This is what all the festivals this month are about: finding light in the darkness. The one thing you may hope for and not get this month is snow. You are far more likely to get snow from February through to March in Britain.

DID YOU KNOW...

In 1647, the English Parliament banned Christmas celebrations. They believed it was wrong to make a party out of such a holy day. Anyone who was seen celebrating was arrested. The ban was lifted in 1660.

FESTIVAL FUN

There's so much festival fun this month, you could be forgiven for thinking that December is one long celebration from start to finish!

21st December *Winter solstice or Midwinter or Yule*

The winter solstice or midwinter falls on the shortest day of the year and has been celebrated in Britain for hundreds of years. Many pagan traditions of Yule have found their way into the celebration of Christmas. At Yule, pagans light candles and fires, decorate their homes with evergreen plants, feast, dance and give gifts. All these things are now traditional at Christmas, too.

Pagans also believe that hanging a sprig of holly near the door brings good luck and keeps away evil spirits. Mistletoe is also hung as a decoration and as a blessing and symbol of new life.

THE YULE LOG

The lighting of the Yule log is the most important part of the Yule festivities. Not only is it believed to conquer the darkness, it is thought to keep away evil spirits and bring good luck for the coming year. Years ago, the log had to be harvested from the householder's land or be given as a gift – it was not bought.

The Yule log would be placed in the fireplace and decorated with evergreen leaves, before cider or ale was poured on it and it was dusted with flour. Then it was lit with a piece of Yule log from the year before and the log would burn for 12 days. Then it was put out and a piece saved for the following year.

Five ways to *Celebrate Midwinter*

★ Go on a walk to gather greenery for your home.
★ Light a fire or a circle of candles.
★ Tell stories around the fire or by candlelight.
★ Have a feast with your favourite food and favourite family and friends!
★ Write down a list of everything you have to be thankful for in the past year.

CHRISTMAS TABLE DECORATIONS

Why not make some homemade Christmas decorations? It's a great thing to do at the beginning of the Christmas holidays when you are trying to pass the time, counting down to Christmas Day – and it's a lot cheaper than buying some! It's always nice to make the dinner table look lovely on Christmas Day. How about making Santa or elf place settings for everyone who is invited?

Make a *Festive Place Setting*

You will need:

Loo rolls or cardboard rolls
Red paper
Green paper
PVA glue

Pompoms in various colours
Black felt-tip pen
Cotton wool
White paper or white sticky labels

1. If you are using cardboard rolls instead of loo rolls, cut them to size. They should be about 10 cm high.
2. Cover the roll in red paper for Santa, or green for the elves.
3. Use glue to fix the paper in place.
4. Use the pompoms to make buttons and noses.
5. Use the black felt-tip pen to draw on the eyes and any other features.
6. Use cotton wool for Santa's beard and the fur trim on his red coat. You can give the elves beards too if you like. Leave some space on their tummies for the next step.
7. Write your guests' or relatives' names on the white paper or sticky labels.
8. Stick these on the tummy area of each of the figures you have made.
9. Decide where everyone is going to sit and put the place settings out so that people can find their place at the table!

DECK THE HALLS!

Decorating the Christmas tree is one of the best things about this time of year. It gets everyone in a Christmassy mood! It's fun getting out the same old decorations, year after year, and remembering where they came from or who gave them to us. But it can be even more fun to make new decorations yourself every year! It's easy to create lovely decorations from recycled material or natural things such as pine cones. So much better than buying more plastic baubles!

Have a go at making these animals:

★ Collect pine cones.
★ Draw eyes on white paper with black pen, then cut them out and stick them on the pine cones to make a hedgehog.
★ Add small sticks for whiskers and string for a tail to make a mouse!
★ Collect teasels, then use small sticks for legs and antlers to make a reindeer.
★ All of these will need string glued or tied around them so that you can hang them on the tree, or you could put them on windowsills around the house to make the whole place more festive.
★ Wooden clothes pegs painted white and decorated with felt-tip pens make lovely snowmen. You can peg these on to the tree or string them together and use them to hold up Christmas cards in rows from the ceiling.

Recipe for *Reindeer Cupcakes*

Lots of people are not keen on mince pies at Christmas, but most people won't be able to resist these tasty alternatives!

You will need:

12-hole muffin tray
Paper muffin cases
Food processor
Sieve
Wire rack
Saucepan
Wooden spoon
Whisk
Knife

150 g dark chocolate (70% cocoa solids)
125 g butter, softened
175 g caster sugar
2 eggs
200 g self-raising flour
2 tablespoons of cocoa powder
100 ml milk
3 tablespoons of double cream
Mini marshmallows, sliced
Black writing icing
Mini pretzels
Giant chocolate buttons

1. *Preheat the oven to 180°C/fan 160°C/Gas Mark 3.*
2. *Line the 12-hole muffin tray with paper muffin cases.*
3. *Melt 100 g of the dark chocolate in the saucepan over a gentle heat and set to one side.*
4. *Beat the butter and sugar together in the food processor until the mixture is light and creamy.*
5. *Gradually beat in the eggs.*
6. *Sift the flour and cocoa powder in the sieve and add this to the mixture, mixing well.*
7. *Pour in the milk and mix gently.*
8. *Spoon the mixture into the muffin cases and bake for 20–25 minutes.*
9. *Remove the cakes from the tin and cool on the wire rack.*
10. *Gently heat the remaining 50 g of chocolate and the cream in the saucepan until the chocolate has melted.*
11. *Whisk the mixture until it is smooth and set it aside to cool slightly.*
12. *Spread the mixture over the top of the cupcakes.*
13. *Finish off with two slices of marshmallow as the eyes and use the black writing icing for the pupils. Stick on pretzels for antlers and a chocolate button for the nose.*

25th December *Christmas Day*

The word Christmas comes from the Anglo-Saxon words *Cristes Mæsse*. It is the Christian celebration of the birth of Jesus Christ. In fact, his birth date is unknown. However, Christians wanted a day to celebrate their belief that Jesus brought goodness and light into the world. As there were already 'light festivals' at this time of year, such as Yule, it made sense to have Christmas then as well.

Saturnalia is an ancient Roman festival that probably influenced how and when Christmas is celebrated. It was dedicated to the god Saturn. All work and business stopped during the festival, and slaves were given a few days of freedom. People said *"Lo Saturnalia!"* to each other the way people today might say "Happy Christmas!" or "Happy Hanukkah!" At the end of the festival people would make presents of candles to one another or wax models of fruit.

31st December *New Year's Eve or Hogmanay*

It is the last day of the year! Just before midnight, it is traditional to turn on a radio or television to follow the countdown of the last few minutes of the old year and to watch the display of fireworks over the River Thames in London. At this point, people often hug and kiss and start to sing the song 'Auld Lang Syne' – although they often don't know the words! Here they are so that you can sing them this year:

> "Should auld acquaintance be forgot,
> and never brought to mind?
> Should auld acquaintance be forgot
> and auld lang syne?
> For auld lang syne my dear,
> for auld lang syne.
> We'll tak'a cup o' kindness yet,
> for auld lang syne."

The words were written by the Scottish poet Robert Burns in 1788. The song asks if it's right to forget old friends and things that have happened in the past.

Just After Midnight . . .

In Scotland, New Year's Eve is known as Hogmanay. If you're lucky enough to be in Scotland on 31st December (and you're allowed to stay up on New Year's Eve until after midnight!) you might be able to join in with the tradition of first-footing.

DID YOU KNOW...

In England and Scotland, New Year's Day used to be 25th March. Scotland made 1st January New Year's Day in 1660 and England followed in 1752.

The 'first foot' to come in through the front door after the last stroke of midnight is supposed to bring good luck. The 'first-footer' should be carrying a piece of coal, some bread, salt and a small drink (known as a 'wee dram'). These items are thought to bring warmth, good food, long life and good cheer for the year ahead.

OUT IN THE WILD

While we humans are busy huddling by the fire and staying warm and cosy, nature carries on working. If you have had enough of being stuck indoors, get your family out on a nature walk. Wrap up warm and keep your eyes peeled. It might be winter, but there's still lots to see!

Robins are very busy at this time of year singing to protect their territories and finding food.

Listen out as the sun goes down and you might hear tawny owls calling to one another. The female calls out, "Too-wit," and the male answers her, "Too-whoo!"

Go for a walk around a river estuary. Birds flock to these places in the winter as the water does not freeze so there is always a lot of food to be found. You might even see a kingfisher or an otter.

Foxes are out hunting in the early evening. They can often be seen slinking into hedges or scurrying down driveways just after the sun has set.

Go for a walk by the sea. This is a great time of year to search the empty beaches for treasures – strange twisted lumps of driftwood, shells, pebbles and seed pods can all be used to make beautiful decorations.

Walk in the woods, too! Collect holly and ivy and pine cones and twigs and then come home and have fun making natural decorations for the house.

VISIT A LONELY NEIGHBOUR

Christmas is a lovely time to get together and share good things. It can be even more rewarding if you can find the time to do this with people you would not normally spend time with.

Do you know someone near you who might be lonely at this time

of year? Perhaps you know an elderly neighbour who doesn't have family nearby? Why not ask a grown-up in your family if you can go round and pay a visit? Or ask if you could invite the neighbour round to your house for a cup of tea and one of your homemade reindeer cupcakes?

WRAPPING UP THE YEAR

"There is a time for everything, and a season for every activity under the heavens."

(ECCLESIASTES 3, FOUND IN THE HEBREW *TANAKH* AND THE *BIBLE*)

So, it's time to say goodbye to the old and make way for the new. Maybe you'll make those New Year's resolutions all over again . . . and just maybe you'll do better at keeping them in 2022! Whatever you do, and wherever you are, thank you for reading this book and

HAPPY NEW YEAR TO YOU AND YOUR FRIENDS AND FAMILY!

CALENDAR 2021

JANUARY

Mo	Tu	We	Th	Fr	Sa	Su
				1	2	3
4	5	6	7	8	9	10
11	12	13	14	15	16	17
18	19	20	21	22	23	24
25	26	27	28	29	30	31

Phases of the Moon

6: 13: 20: 28:

FEBRUARY

Mo	Tu	We	Th	Fr	Sa	Su
1	2	3	4	5	6	7
8	9	10	11	12	13	14
15	16	17	18	19	20	21
22	23	24	25	26	27	28

Phases of the Moon

4: 11: 19: 27:

MARCH

Mo	Tu	We	Th	Fr	Sa	Su
1	2	3	4	5	6	7
8	9	10	11	12	13	14
15	16	17	18	19	20	21
22	23	24	25	26	27	28
29	30	31				

Phases of the Moon

6: ◑ 13: ● 21: ◐ 28: ○

APRIL

Mo	Tu	We	Th	Fr	Sa	Su
			1	2	3	4
5	6	7	8	9	10	11
12	13	14	15	16	17	18
19	20	21	22	23	24	25
26	27	28	29	30		

Phases of the Moon

4: ◑ 12: ● 20: ◐ 27: ○

MAY

Mo	Tu	We	Th	Fr	Sa	Su
					1	2
3	4	5	6	7	8	9
10	11	12	13	14	15	16
17	18	19	20	21	22	23
24	25	26	27	28	29	30
31						

Phases of the Moon

3: ● 11: ● 19: ● 26: ●

JUNE

Mo	Tu	We	Th	Fr	Sa	Su
	1	2	3	4	5	6
7	8	9	10	11	12	13
14	15	16	17	18	19	20
21	22	23	24	25	26	27
28	29	30				

Phases of the Moon

2: ● 10: ● 18: ● 24: ●

JULY

Mo	Tu	We	Th	Fr	Sa	Su
			1	2	3	4
5	6	7	8	9	10	11
12	13	14	15	16	17	18
19	20	21	22	23	24	25
26	27	28	29	30	31	

Phases of the Moon

1: ◑ 10: ● 17: ◑ 24: ○ 31: ◑

AUGUST

Mo	Tu	We	Th	Fr	Sa	Su
						1
2	3	4	5	6	7	8
9	10	11	12	13	14	15
16	17	18	19	20	21	22
23	24	25	26	27	28	29
30	31					

Phases of the Moon

8: ● 15: ◑ 22: ○ 30: ◑

SEPTEMBER

Mo	Tu	We	Th	Fr	Sa	Su
		1	2	3	4	5
6	7	8	9	10	11	12
13	14	15	16	17	18	19
20	21	22	23	24	25	26
27	28	29	30			

Phases of the Moon

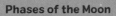

7: ● 13: ◐ 21: ○ 29: ◑

OCTOBER

Mo	Tu	We	Th	Fr	Sa	Su
				1	2	3
4	5	6	7	8	9	10
11	12	13	14	15	16	17
18	19	20	21	22	23	24
25	26	27	28	29	30	31

Phases of the Moon

6: ● 13: ◐ 20: ○ 28: ◑

NOVEMBER

Mo	Tu	We	Th	Fr	Sa	Su
1	2	3	4	5	6	7
8	9	10	11	12	13	14
15	16	17	18	19	20	21
22	23	24	25	26	27	28
29	30					

Phases of the Moon

4: ● 11: ◐ 19: ○ 27: ◑

DECEMBER

Mo	Tu	We	Th	Fr	Sa	Su
		1	2	3	4	5
6	7	8	9	10	11	12
13	14	15	16	17	18	19
20	21	22	23	24	25	26
27	28	29	30	31		

Phases of the Moon

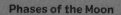
4: ● 11: ◐ 19: ○ 27: ◑

NOTES

GLOSSARY

Advent The period leading up to Christmas

All Saints' Eve A Christian festival to remember saints and loved ones who have died

Allah The name of God for Muslims and Arab Christians

Anglo-Saxons People who lived in Great Britain from 410 until 1066

Apple Day A celebration of apples and orchards

April Fool's Day The first day of April, when people play jokes on each other

Ascension Day A Christian holy day to celebrate the day Jesus rose into heaven

Ash Wednesday The beginning of Lent

Beltane An ancient pagan festival that celebrates the return of summer

Bible The Christian holy book

Birthday Honours The titles given to people on the Queen's official birthday

Birth flower A flower linked to the month of a person's birth

Birthstone A gemstone linked to the month of a person's birth

Blue moon A second full moon in a calendar month

Buddhist Someone who believes in and follows the teachings of the Buddha

Burns Night A celebration of the Scottish poet Robert Burns

Candlemas A Christian festival celebrating the first time that baby Jesus was taken to the temple

Catholic Someone who follows a branch of Christianity led by the Pope

Chinese New Year A colourful celebration of the start of the Chinese year, also known as the 'Spring Festival'

Christian Someone who follows the religion of Christianity and believes in God, Jesus Christ and the teachings of the *Bible*

Church The Christian place of worship

Crop circle A pattern made by flattening crops in a field, usually done overnight

Diwali A Hindu festival of lights to celebrate the victory of light over darkness

Easter A Christian festival to remember the death and return to life of Jesus Christ

Eid al-Adha Also known as the 'Sacrifice Feast', this Islamic festival honours Ibrahim's willingness to obey Allah and marks the end of the *Hajj* pilgrimage to Mecca

Eid al-Fitr Also known as the 'Festival of the Breaking of the Fast', this Islamic festival is a three-day celebration to mark the end of Ramadan

Equator An imaginary line drawn around the middle of the Earth at an equal distance from the north and south poles

Epiphany A Christian holy day, held in January, which marks the end of the Christmas period

Equinox The time twice a year when the length of day and night is exactly equal

Eta Aquariids A meteor shower formed by particles of dust left behind by Halley's Comet

Fast To spend a period of time without eating or drinking

Fertility The ability to create children or young

First-footing A Scottish New Year's tradition, where the 'first footer' is the first person to walk through the door after midnight

First quarter One quarter of the way through the moon's cycle, when we can see exactly half of the moon's face

Fossil The remains or traces of an ancient living thing that has been preserved in rock

Full moon When the entire face of the moon is lit up by the sun's rays

Ganesh Chaturthi A 10-day Hindu festival to worship the god Ganesha

Gemstone A precious or semi-precious stone

Ghee a type of clear butter used in South Asian cooking

Guy Fawkes A member of a group of English Catholics who tried to assassinate King James in 1604 by blowing up the Houses of Parliament

Hanukkah An eight-day 'festival of lights' celebrated by Jewish people, to remember how the Jewish army freed Jerusalem and took back the temple, which they re-dedicated to God

Harvest Gathering crops

Hemisphere Half of the Earth, divided into northern and southern hemispheres by the equator

Hibernate When an animal or plant goes to sleep for the winter

Hindu Someone who follows the South Asian religion of Hinduism, involving the belief in reincarnation and the worship of many gods

Hogmanay The Scottish word for the last day of the year

Holi A Hindu spring festival in celebration of the god Krishna

Holy Spirit Christians believe God exists in three forms at the same time, as God in heaven, as Jesus Christ in heaven, and as the Holy Spirit, which is everywhere

Imbolc A pagan festival marking the beginning of spring

Isra and Mi'raj An Islamic celebration of the Prophet Muhammad's journey from Mecca to Jerusalem and his journey into heaven, when Allah revealed to Muhammad that Muslims should pray five times a day

Jain Someone who follows the ancient Indian religion of Jainism that teaches *ahimsa* (non-violence) to all living creatures

Jerusalem The capital city of Israel, believed to be holy by Jews, Christians and Muslims

Jew Someone who follows the religion of Judaism and believes in God, the Hebrew prophets and the teachings of the *Torah*

Lammas A pagan celebration of the first harvest

Last quarter Three quarters of the way through the moon's cycle, when we can see exactly half of the moon's face

Leap year A year with 366 days in it, which occurs once every four years

Lent A Christian period of fasting in the run-up to Easter

Litha The Anglo-Saxon word for midsummer

Lohri A Punjabi midwinter festival celebrated by Sikhs and Hindus

Lughnasadh A Gaelic festival celebrating the beginning of the harvest season

Maia The Greek goddess of fertility

Matzo A flatbread that Jewish people eat at Passover

May Day The first day of May, celebrated by dancing and singing

Mecca The holiest city of Islam

Meteor A fiery streak in the sky, created when dust and rocks from the tail of a comet pass through the Earth's atmosphere

Michaelmas A Christian festival held at the end of September to honour the angels

Midsummer The longest day and the shortest night of the year, also known as the summer solstice

Midwinter The shortest day and the longest night of the year, also known as the winter solstice

Migrate To move from one place to another

Morris dancing A form of English folk dance with music

Mosque The Islamic place of worship

Muhammad The Muslim Prophet and founder of Islam

Murmuration When hundreds or thousands of starlings fly together in a flowing pattern

Muslim Someone who follows the religion of Islam and believes in Allah, the Prophet Muhammad, the five pillars of Islam and the teachings of the *Qur'an*

Neap tide A tide that happens twice a month, when the difference between high tide and low tide is at its lowest

New moon The first phase in the moon's cycle, when just a very thin crescent shape is visible at night

Old Testament The first part of the *Bible*, originally written in Hebrew

Ostara A pagan festival which is celebrated at the spring equinox

Pagan A follower of paganism, a pre-Christian religion, who believes in many gods and goddesses

Passover A Jewish celebration to remember how Moses helped the Israelites escape from Egypt

Pentecost A Christian festival on the seventh Sunday after Easter, to celebrate the day after his death when Jesus returned to his disciples in the form of the Holy Spirit

Promised Land The land that Jewish people believe was given by God to Abraham and his descendants

Purification The process of making something or someone clean

Purim A Jewish holiday in memory of when the Jewish people were saved from a cruel man called Haman

Qur'an The Islamic holy book

Raksha Bandhan A Hindu festival that celebrates the relationship between brothers and sisters

Ramadan A month when Muslims hold a fast during the hours of daylight to become closer to Allah, and to remember the time that the Qur'an was first revealed to the Prophet Muhammad

Resolution A decision to do, or not do something

Samhain Eve A pagan festival for giving thanks at the end of the harvest

Sea Sunday The day when Christians pray for sailors and their families

Seder A special Jewish feast to celebrate the beginning of Passover

Shavuot A Jewish holiday to remember the day that God gave Moses the Torah

Shrove Tuesday The day before the Christian period of fasting called Lent begins, also known as 'Pancake Day'

Sikh Someone who follows the religion of Sikhism and believes in the writings and teachings of the Ten Sikh Gurus

Spring tide A tide just after a new or full moon, when the difference between high tide and low tide is at its highest

Swan Upping An annual ceremony in which mute swans are taken from the River Thames to be counted and marked to identify them, before being released

Synagogue The Jewish place of worship

Ten Commandments A list of laws or rules that Christians and Jews follow that they believe were given by God to Moses

Tide The rising and falling of the sea

Torah The Jewish holy book

Trooping the colour A ceremony performed to celebrate the Queen's birthday

Tu B'Shevat Jewish New Year, also known as the 'New Year for Trees'

Twelfth Night A festival some Christians celebrate to mark the coming of the Epiphany

Wassailing A pagan tradition of blessing the apple trees in the new year

Whitsun Another name for the Christian festival of Pentecost

Yom Kippur A Jewish holiday for saying sorry for things you have done wrong and asking for forgiveness

Yule A pagan festival held in midwinter to celebrate the winter solstice

INDEX